62 DAYS OF DEVOTIONS BASED ON THE BOOK OF PROVERBS

wisdom
for
living

S E L W

CWR

Copyright © CWR 2010. Text written by Selwyn Hughes and previously published by CWR
in 1991 as *Every Day with Jesus, The Seven Pillars of Wisdom*. Revised and updated 2008 by
Mick Brooks as *Every Day with Jesus, Wisdom for Living*.

CWR, Waverley Abbey House, Waverley Lane, Farnham, Surrey GU9 8EP, UK
Tel: 01252 784700 Email: mail@cwr.org.uk Registered Charity No. 294387. Registered
Limited Company No. 1990308.

Unless otherwise stated all Scripture quotations are from the HCSB, Holman Christian
Standard Bible® © Copyright 1999, 2000, 2002, 2003 by Holman Bible Publishers. Used
by permission. Holman Christian Standard Bible®, Holman CSB® and HCSB® are federally
registered trademarks of Holman Bible Publishers.

Cover image: CWR
Printed in China by 1010 Printing
ISBN: 978-1-85345-558-2

A word of introduction

Who doesn't want to live well? The vast majority of us hope to experience life to the full and make the best of each opportunity that arises in our hoped for three score years and ten. This drive has, in recent years, spawned the bestselling category of self-help books, DVDs and audio resources. I recently searched the internet for 'rules for living', and found nearly 13 million results, including over 50 book titles published in the UK alone. All seek to answer this question: 'What are the rules for living?'

There is, it seems, an abundance of philosophies and lifestyle advice out there on how to live life well. The difficulty, however, is that much of the advice offered is, at times, contradictory, and we can find ourselves drifting through a pluralist world, uncertain of our direction.

Selwyn leads us through the book of Proverbs, introducing us to God's wisdom for living. Over the years, I have noticed that many Christians have one thing in common. Whatever their circumstances – whether they are young, old, running from one thing to the next or frail, maybe even housebound – each has a vitality about them that shapes a playful twinkle in their eye. They exude a sense of energy and a love of life. These things, however, don't come from following a set of rules, or even a set of principles, but from following a Person – following Jesus. He's the One who has gone before us, who has lived life to the full and even conquered death. What better way is there to live than to follow Him?

These wise words first appeared as an issue of the daily Bible-reading notes *Every Day with Jesus* written by Selwyn Hughes. It was my privilege to take on the role of Consulting Editor of *Every Day with Jesus* following Selwyn's death in 2006. We received so many encouraging comments, responses and requests to re-publish this material that we have chosen to make it available in book form.

We have included the full relevant Bible text for each day, with the key verse for the day highlighted in bold for clarity, and also included the entire text of Proverbs for reading/reference.

Mick Brooks

Mick Brooks
CWR

Wisdom is our
   rock to build on –
   truth to live by –
   outstretched hand –
   worthy goal –
   word of hope –
   united hearts –
   path to purity.
Wisdom
   leads to eternity
      with God.
Eternity begins now.

Susan Lenzkes © 2007
Used by permission

DAY 01

Wise up and live
FOR READING & MEDITATION – PROVERBS 1:1–19

¹ The proverbs of Solomon son of David, king of Israel:

² **For gaining wisdom and being instructed;**
for understanding insightful sayings;

³ for receiving wise instruction
[in] righteousness, justice, and integrity;
⁴ for teaching shrewdness to the inexperienced,
knowledge and discretion to a young man—
⁵ a wise man will listen and increase his learning,
and a discerning man will obtain guidance—
⁶ for understanding a proverb or a parable,
the words of the wise, and their riddles.
⁷ The fear of the LORD
is the beginning of knowledge;
fools despise wisdom and instruction.

⁸ Listen, my son, to your father's instruction,
and don't reject your mother's teaching,
⁹ for they will be a garland of grace on your head
and a [gold] chain around your neck.
¹⁰ My son, if sinners entice you,
don't be persuaded.
¹¹ If they say—"Come with us!
Let's set an ambush and kill someone.
Let's attack some innocent person just for fun!
¹² Let's swallow them alive, like Sheol,
still healthy as they go down to the Pit.
¹³ We'll find all kinds of valuable property
and fill our houses with plunder.
¹⁴ Throw in your lot with us,
and we'll all share our money" —
¹⁵ my son, don't travel that road with them
or set foot on their path,
¹⁶ because their feet run toward trouble
and they hurry to commit murder.

¹⁷ It is foolish to spread a net
   where any bird can see it,
¹⁸ but they set an ambush to kill themselves;
   they attack their own lives.
¹⁹ Such are the paths of all who pursue gain dishonestly;
   it takes the lives of those who profit from it.

WE ARE GOING to set out to explore some of the great and thrilling themes of the book of Proverbs. I was introduced to it within weeks of becoming a Christian, and I have no hesitation in saying that, as far as practical matters are concerned, it has influenced my thinking and coloured my judgments more than any other book of the Bible.

I shall never forget my pastor taking me aside just after I had been converted and telling me, 'I am going to teach you to steal, to drink, to lie and to swear.' Looking at my expression, and seeing my astonishment, he quickly went on to say, 'I want to teach you how to steal time out of every day to read something from the book of Proverbs. And then I want to teach you how to drink from its clear, refreshing waters, to lie on your bed at night and meditate on its great themes, and to swear that by the grace of God you will put into practice its wonderful teaching.' My pastor's rather novel approach laid deep in my mind the importance of this powerful book, and the truths I have learned from it I now long to share with you.

We begin with the question: What is the purpose of Proverbs? Our text for today gives us the clue. Listen to how the Living Bible paraphrases it: 'He [Solomon] wrote them to teach his people how to live – how to act in every circumstance ...' This, then, is what Proverbs is all about – wisdom for living. Millions of people know how to make a living but do not know how to live. They know everything about life except how to live it. I tell you, the more you understand the book of Proverbs, and the more you put its truths and principles into practice, the more effective will be your living. I guarantee it.

PRAYER

O FATHER, help me come to grips with the wisdom that enables me not just to live, but to live abundantly. I long to know what I need to do to get on in life. Through the ancient but inspired words of Proverbs please teach me how. Amen.

Wisdom personified

FOR READING & MEDITATION – PROVERBS 1:20–33

²⁰ Wisdom calls out in the street;
she raises her voice in the public squares.
²¹ She cries out above the commotion;
she speaks at the entrance of the city gates:
²² "How long, foolish ones, will you love ignorance?
[How long] will [you] mockers enjoy mocking
and [you] fools hate knowledge?
²³ If you turn to my discipline,
then I will pour out my spirit on you
and teach you my words.
²⁴ Since I called out and you refused,
extended my hand and no one paid attention,
²⁵ since you neglected all my counsel
and did not accept my correction,
²⁶ I, in turn, will laugh at your calamity.
I will mock when terror strikes you,
²⁷ when terror strikes you like a storm
and your calamity comes like a whirlwind,
when trouble and stress overcome you.
²⁸ Then they will call me, but I won't answer;
they will search for me, but won't find me.
²⁹ Because they hated knowledge,
didn't choose to fear the LORD,
³⁰ were not interested in my counsel,
and rejected all my correction,
³¹ they will eat the fruit of their way
and be glutted with their own schemes.
³² For the waywardness of the inexperienced will kill them,
and the complacency of fools will destroy them.

³³ **But whoever listens to me will live securely**
and be free from the fear of danger."

BEFORE SETTLING DOWN to focus on our theme, which is Wisdom for Living, it will be helpful if we acquaint ourselves with some background information concerning the book – hence these opening days will be more of an introduction to the book than an exposition of it.

You will not get far when reading Proverbs before you begin to notice that both wisdom and its opposite, foolishness, are personified as women – Lady Wisdom and Lady Folly – each of whom attempts to persuade people to follow her ways. This personification of wisdom and of folly is a literary device that the writer uses to add punch and power to his points, particularly in the first nine chapters. We use a similar form of expression when we personify natural laws and refer to them as 'Mother Nature'. For example, we may hear people comment, 'Mother Nature is bringing out the spring flowers early', or, 'Mother Nature is doing her thing'. This is a poetic and colourful way of referring to the principles and laws that govern the universe in which we live.

Notice how wisdom is personified in these words taken from the passage we have read today: 'Wisdom calls out in the street; she raises her voice in the public squares. She cries out above the commotion; she speaks at the entrance of the city gates' (vv.20–21). Later on in the book of Proverbs you will see how similar language is used of Lady Folly. The purpose of this personification is to make the reader vividly aware that over and against the fatal attraction of folly, wisdom brings security and contentment. Wisdom is the soul's true bride and true counsellor. Wisdom is good for us; it is what our personalities were designed for by God Himself.

PRAYER

O Father, help me to grasp the truth that I am made for a certain way of living – Your way – and when I try to live against that way then I am nothing but a fool. Make me wise, dear Lord, with the wisdom that comes from You. Amen.

DAY 03

The source of all wisdom

FOR READING & MEDITATION – PROVERBS 2:12–22

¹² **rescuing you from the way of evil—**
from the one who says perverse things,

¹³ [from] those who abandon the right paths
to walk in ways of darkness,

¹⁴ [from] those who enjoy doing evil
and celebrate perversity,

¹⁵ whose paths are crooked,
and whose ways are devious.

¹⁶ It will rescue you from a forbidden woman,
from a stranger with her flattering talk,

¹⁷ who abandons the companion of her youth
and forgets the covenant of her God;

¹⁸ for her house sinks down to death
and her ways to the land of the departed spirits.

¹⁹ None return who go to her;
none reach the paths of life.

²⁰ So follow the way of good people,
and keep to the paths of the righteous.

²¹ For the upright will inhabit the land,
and those of integrity will remain in it;

²² but the wicked will be cut off from the land,
and the treacherous uprooted from it.

YESTERDAY WE TOUCHED on the thought that in the book of Proverbs, particularly in the first nine chapters, wisdom and foolishness are seen as persons. Jesus was also using the device of personification when He concluded His address to the crowds on the significance of John the Baptist with the words, 'Yet wisdom is vindicated by her deeds' (Matt. 11:19). Some have expressed the view that the personification of wisdom in the Scriptures indicates that wisdom is to be seen as a person, perhaps a member of the angelic hierarchy, who visits men and women and imparts divine wisdom to them. But this, in my opinion, is taking things too far. The writer is simply using a literary device to make a point.

Having said that, however, most evangelical commentators are agreed that the device of personification when used in connection with wisdom is to prepare the way for the apostle Paul's great statement in 1 Corinthians 1:24, namely that Christ is 'God's power and God's wisdom'. If this is so then it suggests that the divine purpose underlying the personification of wisdom in the book of Proverbs is not simply to acquaint us with an absorbing set of guidelines or helpful suggestions by which to run our lives, but to hint that true wisdom lies in a Person – that Person being none other than Jesus Christ.

The Christian message moves beyond the wise proverbs of Solomon, which, by the way, commend themselves to non-Christians as well as Christians, and points to the fact that the highest wisdom comes from a relationship with the One who is the fount of all wisdom – Jesus. Knowing the principles of wisdom is one thing; knowing the Person in whom all wisdom resides is another.

PRAYER

O Father, how can I sufficiently thank You that by faith I am linked to the source of all wisdom – the Lord Jesus Christ? Let the wonder of this relationship – that I am in Him and He is in me – sink deep into my soul today. Amen.

DAY 04

Sophomores – 'wise fools'

FOR READING & MEDITATION – PROVERBS 4:1–9

¹ Listen, [my] sons, to a father's discipline,
and pay attention so that you may gain understanding,
² for I am giving you good instruction.
Don't abandon my teaching.
³ When I was a son with my father,
tender and precious to my mother,
⁴ he taught me and said:
"Your heart must hold on to my words.
Keep my commands and live.
⁵ Get wisdom, get understanding;
don't forget or turn away from the words of my mouth.

⁶ **Don't abandon wisdom, and she will watch over you;**
love her, and she will guard you.

⁷ Wisdom is supreme—so get wisdom.
And whatever else you get, get understanding.
⁸ Cherish her, and she will exalt you;
if you embrace her, she will honor you.
⁹ She will place a garland of grace on your head;
she will give you a crown of beauty."

HAVING SEEN WHY the writer of Proverbs uses the device of personification in connection with wisdom, and having understood that the main message of the book is to provide us with wisdom for living, it is time now to ask ourselves: What exactly is wisdom? How is it to be defined?

Some say wisdom is synonymous with knowledge and use the two words interchangeably. There is, however, a world of difference between knowledge and wisdom, as writers and philosophers down the ages have pointed out. Knowledge is the capacity to comprehend and retain what we are taught; wisdom is the ability to put that knowledge to best effect. If knowledge is the same thing as wisdom then, as Paul Larsen points out, 'There are many "wise" men who are fools.' Schools and universities cram information into the minds of the students who attend them, and so they graduate knowing a good deal about such matters as the solar system, microbiology, history, psychology, the laws of physics, art, and so on. However, knowledge by itself does not stop them from making a mess of their lives. In the United States a second-year university or high school student is called a 'sophomore', a term derived from the Greek words for 'wise' and 'foolish' – in other words, a 'wise fool'. How revealing! When we reach the higher stages of education we think that we know it all, but if this attitude is not changed then we will soon demonstrate what it means to be a fool.

A 'fool' in Proverbs is not someone who can't pass a simple literacy or numeracy test; it is someone who thinks they know what life is all about but does not. Those whom the world recognises as 'wise' may, from heaven's standpoint, be the biggest fools.

PRAYER

Father, I begin to understand what Paul meant when he said 'we are fools for Christ'. My lifestyle may appear foolish to those around me, but help me never to forget that if I am following Your principles it is the highest wisdom. Amen.

DAY 05
The 'wisdom literature'

FOR READING & MEDITATION – PROVERBS 5:15–23

¹⁵ Drink water from your own cistern,
water flowing from your own well.
¹⁶ Should your springs flow in the streets,
streams of water in the public squares?
¹⁷ They should be for you alone
and not for you [to share] with strangers.
¹⁸ Let your fountain be blessed,
and take pleasure in the wife of your youth.
¹⁹ A loving doe, a graceful fawn—
let her breasts always satisfy you;
be lost in her love forever.
²⁰ Why, my son, would you be infatuated
with a forbidden woman
or embrace the breast of a stranger?

²¹ **For a man's ways are before the LORD's eyes,
and He considers all his paths.**

²² A wicked man's iniquities entrap him;
he is entangled in the ropes of his own sin.
²³ He will die because there is no instruction,
and be lost because of his great stupidity.

THERE ARE JUST a few more important general points to make concerning Proverbs before we start to focus on our theme – Wisdom for Living. Proverbs is a book considered to be part of the 'wisdom literature' of the Old Testament. These books are associated with a class of people called 'wise men' or 'sages'. Wise men were highly regarded both in Israel and in the surrounding nations, as 1 Kings 4:34 reveals.

The Old Testament consists of three sections: first, the Law, second, the Prophets, and third, the Writings – answering to the three groups of leaders outlined in Jeremiah 18:18: '… for the law will never be lost from the *priest*, or counsel from the *wise*, or an oracle from the *prophet*.' Included within the category of the Writings are the wisdom books – Job, Psalms, Proverbs, Ecclesiastes and Song of Songs. While the prophets and the priests dealt with the religious life of Israel, the wise men were called upon to give advice about more philosophical matters. They were the ones who made the point that the world was designed for wisdom, and those who followed wisdom would find that the world was made for them.

The book of Proverbs, which was largely written by Solomon, whose wisdom was legendary, is crammed with the best advice it is possible to get, and it is a tragedy that it is not part of our educational system. But perhaps a greater tragedy is the fact that in some parts of the Christian community (though not all) Proverbs is an unexplored book. I do not hesitate to say that any church that does not encourage its people, especially its young people, to delve into the book of Proverbs is doing them a major disservice.

PRAYER

Gracious Father, help me develop a love for Your wisdom literature. Grant that these days of searching and exploring may result in a new understanding of wisdom, and that new evidences of Your wisdom may be seen in my life. Amen.

DAY 06
'Portable medicine'
FOR READING & MEDITATION – PROVERBS 28:1–17

¹ The wicked flee when no one is pursuing [them],
but the righteous are as bold as a lion.

² When a land is in rebellion, it has many rulers,
but with a discerning and knowledgeable person,
it endures.

³ A destitute leader who oppresses the poor
is like a driving rain that leaves no food.

⁴ Those who reject the law praise the wicked,
but those who keep the law battle against them.

⁵ Evil men do not understand justice,
but those who seek the LORD understand everything.

⁶ Better a poor man who lives with integrity
than a rich man who distorts right and wrong.

⁷ A discerning son keeps the law,
but a companion of gluttons humiliates his father.

⁸ Whoever increases his wealth through excessive interest
collects it for one who is kind to the poor.

⁹ Anyone who turns his ear away from hearing the law—
even his prayer is detestable.

¹⁰ The one who leads the upright into an evil way
will fall into his own pit,
but the blameless will inherit what is good.

¹¹ A rich man is wise in his own eyes,
but a poor man who has discernment sees through him.

¹² When the righteous triumph,
there is great rejoicing,
but when the wicked come to power,
people hide themselves.

¹³ The one who conceals his sins
will not prosper,
but whoever confesses and renounces them
will find mercy.

¹⁴ Happy is the one who is always reverent,
   but one who hardens his heart falls into trouble.
¹⁵ A wicked ruler over a helpless people
   is like a roaring lion or a charging bear.
¹⁶ A leader who lacks understanding
   is very oppressive,
   but one who hates unjust gain
   prolongs his life.
¹⁷ A man burdened by bloodguilt
   will be a fugitive until death.
   Let no one help him.

YESTERDAY WE ENDED with the comment that any church which does not encourage its people, especially its young people, to delve into the book of Proverbs is doing them a major disservice. Earlier I mentioned that I was introduced to Proverbs when I myself was young – within weeks of becoming a Christian, in fact. Now, several decades later, I can testify that this book, perhaps more than any other in the Bible, has supplied me with wisdom for living and has enriched my life. What is more, the teaching in this book has greatly empowered both my ministry and my writing. Every child, young adult, man and woman needs to be steeped in the book of Proverbs as there is nothing to be found in literature that can so prepare them for life.

Alexander Maclaren, a famous preacher from a past generation, said, 'Proverbs is portable medicine for the fevers of youth.' How true. And, as with any medicine, what matters is that you take it whether or not you know the doctor who prescribed it. A number of young men and women known to me have told me that they came to faith in Jesus Christ through reading the book of Proverbs. One said to me, 'When I applied the principles of Proverbs, and saw that these wise and witty sayings really worked, I was drawn to search for the One whose hand was so clearly present in the book and also in my life. After reading the instruction manual I wanted to know the Instructor.'

Not everyone, of course, will react in that way. However, I myself am convinced that encouraging and exposing people, especially the young, to the wise sayings and principles found in the book of Proverbs is one of the greatest forms of outreach that can be conducted.

PRAYER

O Father, help me use any influence I have with the young to motivate them to read and absorb what is found in the book of Proverbs. But, first, let me dwell deep within it myself. In Jesus' name I pray. Amen.

'Invoked or not ...'

FOR READING & MEDITATION – PROVERBS 8:12–36

12 I, Wisdom, share a home with shrewdness
and have knowledge and discretion.
13 To fear the LORD is to hate evil.
I hate arrogant pride, evil conduct,
and perverse speech.
14 I possess good advice and competence;
I have understanding and strength.
15 It is by me that kings reign
and rulers enact just law;
16 by me, princes lead,
as do nobles [and] all righteous judges.
17 I love those who love me,
and those who search for me find me.
18 With me are riches and honor,
lasting wealth and righteousness.
19 My fruit is better than solid gold,
and my harvest than pure silver.
20 I walk in the way of righteousness,
along the paths of justice,
21 giving wealth as an inheritance to those who love me,
and filling their treasuries.
22 The LORD made me
at the beginning of His creation,
before His works of long ago.
23 I was formed before ancient times,
from the beginning, before the earth began.
24 I was brought forth
when there were no watery depths
and no springs filled with water.
25 I was brought forth
before the mountains and hills were established,
26 before He made the land, the fields,
or the first soil on earth.
27 I was there when He established the heavens,
when He laid out the horizon on the surface of the ocean,

²⁸ when He placed the skies above,
   when the fountains of the ocean gushed forth,
²⁹ when He set a limit for the sea
   so that the waters would not violate His command,
   when He laid out the foundations of the earth.
³⁰ I was a skilled craftsman beside Him.
   I was His delight every day,
   always rejoicing before Him.
³¹ I was rejoicing in His inhabited world,
   delighting in the human race.
³² And now, [my] sons, listen to me;
   those who keep my ways are happy.
³³ Listen to instruction and be wise;
   don't ignore it.

³⁴ **Anyone who listens to me is happy,**

   watching at my doors every day,

   waiting by the posts of my doorway.

³⁵ For the one who finds me finds life
   and obtains favor from the LORD,
³⁶ but the one who sins against me harms himself;
   all who hate me love death."

THE MORE YOU read and study Proverbs, and the more you apply its words to your life, the more you will find that its wise and witty sayings 'work'. They work because God has set things up to work this way. It was said of Carl Jung, the famous psychologist, that written over his study door were these words: 'Invoked or not, God is present.' This interesting statement provides us with a clue to understanding Proverbs, for whether or not men and women invoke the Creator, His creative and sustaining wisdom goes on giving them a world where wisdom operates and where things make sense to humankind.

One person has described Proverbs as 'the scrapbook of common grace'. 'Common grace' is the phrase theologians use to describe the grace that God gives to humanity in general so that, whether they turn to Him or not, they are enabled to live more effectively and wisely on the earth. 'Wisdom,' says Charles G. Martin, 'writes the handbook of instruction in God's workshop, and when people despise wisdom, that is, true wisdom, they blot the copy book of life.'

Of course, we must accept the fact that some may pursue wisdom for the wrong reasons – out of self-interest, for instance, or just because wisdom 'works'. But, as Archbishop William Temple once put it, 'The art of politics is so to arrange matters that self-interest prompts what justice demands.' Leaving aside for the moment the wonderful prospect of heaven, it has to be said that life on earth would be a great deal better if wisdom, rather than folly, prevailed.

PRAYER

Father, I am so thankful for Your 'common grace'. Your love reaches down to help people live life in a sensible and profitable way even though they may never come to know You personally. What a wonderful God You are. Amen.

DAY 08

'Come into my house'

FOR READING & MEDITATION – PROVERBS 9:1–9

> ¹ **Wisdom has built her house;**
> **she has carved out her seven pillars.**

² She has prepared her meat; she has mixed her wine;
she has also set her table.
³ She has sent out her servants;
she calls out from the highest points of the city:
⁴ "Whoever is inexperienced, enter here!"
To the one who lacks sense, she says,
⁵ "Come, eat my bread,
and drink the wine I have mixed.
⁶ Leave inexperience behind, and you will live;
pursue the way of understanding.
⁷ The one who corrects a mocker
will bring dishonor on himself;
the one who rebukes a wicked man will get hurt.
⁸ Don't rebuke a mocker, or he will hate you;
rebuke a wise man, and he will love you.
⁹ Instruct a wise man, and he will be wiser still;
teach a righteous man, and he will learn more.

HAVING LOOKED AT some background information concerning the book of Proverbs, we are ready now to begin focusing on our main theme. As I shall be taking you to different sections and passages of this book, and not covering every single verse, I would encourage you to sit down during the next few days and preferably in two or three sittings, read through the whole of Proverbs, which you will find printed on pages 161–210 of this book. This will prepare you for our daily meditations over the next few weeks.

Our text for today tells us that wisdom is like a house built on seven pillars. There are two main ways of interpreting this verse. One view is that both wisdom and folly have a house to which humankind is invited. Wisdom has a much larger house than folly, being built upon 'seven pillars' – a sign in ancient times of wealth, status and prestige. There is no doubt that this interpretation of the text has much to commend it, but I am going to take a different approach in these studies – namely that wisdom has seven major aspects. The book of Proverbs does not state categorically what these are, so, based on my study and understanding of this great book, my intention is to give you what I consider to be the seven chief aspects of wisdom.

Never in the history of the human race have there been so many problems, so much confusion, and so many conflicting philosophies concerning how to live. Those who lack wisdom do not have the perspectives that enable them to discern the connection between cause and effect, and therefore they don't understand what they are stumbling over, or, if they do avoid problems, they don't understand why they avoid them. We need wisdom to live – and the book of Proverbs will give it to us.

PRAYER

Gracious and loving heavenly Father, my appetite is whetted and now I am ready to begin my study. Grant that as I expose myself to the truths of Your Word, wisdom may become more deeply imprinted upon my spirit. In Jesus' name I pray. Amen.

DAY 09
The ability to trust
FOR READING & MEDITATION – PROVERBS 3:1–18

¹ My son, don't forget my teaching,
  but let your heart keep my commands;
² for they will bring you
  many days, a full life, and well-being.
³ Never let loyalty and faithfulness leave you.
  Tie them around your neck;
  write them on the tablet of your heart.
⁴ Then you will find favor and high regard
  in the sight of God and man.

⁵ **Trust in the LORD with all your heart,**
  and do not rely on your own understanding;

⁶ think about Him in all your ways,
  and He will guide you on the right paths.
⁷ Don't consider yourself to be wise;
  fear the LORD and turn away from evil.
⁸ This will be healing for your body
  and strengthening for your bones.
⁹ Honor the LORD with your possessions
  and with the first produce of your entire harvest;
¹⁰ then your barns will be completely filled,
  and your vats will overflow with new wine.
¹¹ Do not despise the LORD's instruction, my son,
  and do not loathe His discipline;
¹² for the LORD disciplines the one He loves,
  just as a father, the son he delights in.

¹³ Happy is a man who finds wisdom
  and who acquires understanding,
¹⁴ for she is more profitable than silver,
  and her revenue is better than gold.
¹⁵ She is more precious than jewels;
  nothing you desire compares with her.
¹⁶ Long life is in her right hand;
  in her left, riches and honor.

¹⁷ Her ways are pleasant,
   and all her paths, peaceful.
¹⁸ She is a tree of life to those who embrace her,
   and those who hold on to her are happy.

WE TURN NOW to consider the first of what I believe to be the seven key aspects of wisdom – *trust*. The theme of trust occurs throughout Proverbs; it appears in almost every passage and on every page. The word 'trust' itself occurs quite often, the frequency varying according to the translation you read (in the Authorised Version, for example, 'trust' appears nine times). Trust in God is shown in Proverbs to be of far greater value than any human endeavour, however well planned and clever. According to Rabbi Bar Kappa, the verse which is our text for today is the pivot around which all the essential principles of Judaism revolve. He claims that these words summarise the teaching of the whole of the Old Testament and give a clear focus to the fact that the wise are those who trust God and follow His directions for living.

But what exactly is trust? How important is it to daily living? Why does the theme of trust occur so many times, not only in Proverbs but in other parts of Scripture as well? The dictionary defines trust as 'a firm belief in the reliability, honesty, veracity, justice and strength of a person or thing'. Basically, trust is confidence – confidence that what we believe about a person or thing is true.

We tend to think of trust as being a spiritual quality, but actually it is an essential part of life for everyone. It would be very difficult to get through a single day without the exercise of trust. All government, all economics, all institutions, all marriages, and all relationships between people are fundamentally governed by trust. We cannot relate well to God or others unless we have the ability to trust.

PRAYER

Father, I see that trust is an essential thread that runs through the whole of life. Teach me the art of trusting, for an art it is. Help me to relax and maintain complete confidence in You – hour by hour and day by day. Amen.

Trust is good for us

FOR READING & MEDITATION – PROVERBS 14:14–26

14 The disloyal will get what their conduct deserves,
and a good man, what his [deeds deserve].

15 **The inexperienced believe anything,**
but the sensible watch their steps.

16 A wise man is cautious and turns from evil,
but a fool is easily angered and is careless.

17 A quick-tempered man acts foolishly,
and a man who schemes is hated.

18 The gullible inherit foolishness,
but the sensible are crowned with knowledge.

19 The evil bow before those who are good,
the wicked, at the gates of the righteous.

20 A poor man is hated even by his neighbor,
but there are many who love the rich.

21 The one who despises his neighbor sins,
but whoever shows kindness to the poor will be happy.

22 Don't those who plan evil go astray?
But those who plan good find loyalty and faithfulness.

23 There is profit in all hard work,
but endless talk leads only to poverty.

24 The crown of the wise is their wealth,
but the foolishness of fools produces foolishness.

25 A truthful witness rescues lives,
but one who utters lies is deceitful.

26 In the fear of the LORD one has strong confidence
and his children have a refuge.

WE SAW YESTERDAY that all relationships, both human and divine, are fundamentally governed by trust. Without trust, society would deteriorate into paranoia – the feeling that everyone is out to get you. Mental health specialists see an inability to trust as a symptom of emotional ill health. Erik Erikson, a developmental psychologist whose studies on the subject of trust are well known among psychologists, says that the capacity to trust is the foundation of good emotional health, and conditions such as chronic anxiety, nervousness or paranoia could be caused by an inability to trust. Although people may let us down and betray our trust, we must be careful that we do not allow those experiences to lead us to the conclusion that everyone we meet is a conspirator.

On the other hand, you may have come across the expression 'a trusting fool' – a term used to describe a person who is unable to discern any cunning schemes that are being devised to exploit him. Erikson also says, 'Unless we have a balanced approach to life – a basic trust together with a certain degree of caution – then we will never achieve emotional maturity or wholeness.' Please take careful note of his words 'a *balanced* approach to life'. Therein lies the secret. We must learn how to trust while at the same time exercising a certain amount of caution.

Our text for today tells us that 'the inexperienced believe anything'. However, that should not cause us to go to the other extreme and believe that everything people tell us is a lie or a fabrication. The point is that we should not be gullible. Truth is a narrow column and we must watch that we do not lose our balance and fall off.

PRAYER

O Father, help me to be a balanced person – one who stands on the narrow column of truth without falling off into one extreme or the other. Remind me that error is often truth taken to an extreme. Please keep me always in the truth. Amen.

A snake in the grass

FOR READING & MEDITATION – PROVERBS 16:10–20

10 God's verdict is on the lips of a king;
   his mouth should not err in judgment.
11 Honest balances and scales are the LORD's;
   all the weights in the bag are His concern.
12 Wicked behavior is detestable to kings,
   since a throne is established through righteousness.
13 Righteous lips are a king's delight,
   and he loves one who speaks honestly.
14 A king's fury is a messenger of death,
   but a wise man appeases it.
15 When a king's face lights up, there is life;
   his favor is like a cloud with spring rain.
16 Acquire wisdom—
   how much better it is than gold!
   And acquire understanding—
   it is preferable to silver.
17 The highway of the upright avoids evil;
   the one who guards his way protects his life.
18 Pride comes before destruction,
   and an arrogant spirit before a fall.
19 Better to be lowly of spirit with the humble
   than to divide plunder with the proud.
20 **The one who understands a matter finds success,**
   and the one who trusts in the LORD will be happy.

PICKING UP FROM where we were yesterday – talking about the need to maintain a proper balance between trust and caution – we ask ourselves: Why does the Bible present us with the idea of caution? The simple answer is because we live in a fallen world. God made the first human pair perfect in every way and put them in a beautiful garden. They trusted Him for everything they needed and not once did He let them down.

However, there was a 'snake in the grass' who hatched a plot to which they succumbed, and so they were brought down to ruin. Their downfall, in turn, plunged the whole human race into chaos and uncertainty (see Gen. 3).

Because of the Fall, life is beset with problems, especially when it comes to the matter of trust. I can't rely entirely on nature – sometimes it rains too much and at other times not enough. I can't rely entirely on family or friends – sometimes they won't or can't help, and at other times they may help too much. Sin has struck so deeply into human relationships that it would be unwise not to recognise that at times and for a variety of reasons people may let us down.

In one way or another the Fall has played havoc with this issue of trust, but we must be careful that we do not allow the failures of trust we may experience on the human level to affect our view of God. Let me spell it out as clearly as I can: you can put your trust in God without fear of ever being let down. The apostle Peter expresses it like this: '… the one who trusts in him will never be put to shame' (1 Pet. 2:6, NIV). Drop your anchor into the depths of this reassuring and encouraging revelation. Whoever else you may not be able to trust – you can trust your heavenly Father.

PRAYER

O Father, what encouragement this thought gives me: whoever else I cannot trust, I can trust You. I have heard this truth so often and read it so many times; now help me take hold of it. In Jesus' name I pray. Amen.

Why is trust difficult?

FOR READING & MEDITATION – PROVERBS 28:18–28

¹⁸ The one who lives with integrity will be helped,
but one who distorts right and wrong
will suddenly fall.

¹⁹ The one who works his land
will have plenty of food,
but whoever chases fantasies
will have his fill of poverty.

²⁰ A faithful man will have many blessings,
but one in a hurry to get rich
will not go unpunished.

²¹ It is not good to show partiality—
yet a man may sin for a piece of bread.

²² A greedy man is in a hurry for wealth;
he doesn't know that poverty will come to him.

²³ One who rebukes a person will later find more favor
than one who flatters with his tongue.

²⁴ The one who robs his father or mother
and says, "That's no sin,"
is a companion to a man who destroys.

²⁵ A greedy person provokes conflict,
but whoever trusts in the LORD will prosper.

²⁶ **The one who trusts in himself is a fool,**
but one who walks in wisdom will be safe.

²⁷ The one who gives to the poor
will not be in need,
but one who turns his eyes away
will receive many curses.

²⁸ When the wicked come to power,
people hide,
but when they are destroyed,
the righteous flourish.

TODAY WE ASK the question: Why do some people find it so difficult to trust? Many have said to me, 'My problem is I find it so hard to trust.' Something I have observed in talking to people over the years is this: a person who finds it difficult to trust on a human level often finds it difficult to trust on a spiritual level. Let me suggest what I think lies behind the inability to trust.

Trust is a learned response, and we begin learning it the moment we are born. A newborn baby arrives in the world with a great deal of vulnerability, and among other things has to learn the art of developing a basic trust. If the parents are loving, reliable, predictable and trustworthy the child soon gets the idea, 'I can trust these people who are looking after me. They don't always respond the way I would like them to but generally they are there for me when I need them.' If, however, there is no reliable and consistent input of love and affection into a child's personality in the early years, if the parents are perceived as unconcerned and unpredictable, the child gets the idea, 'People are not to be trusted'. And in cases where parents are not just unconcerned, but are unkind and even abusive, then the development of a basic trust is hard – some would say impossible.

My experience in counselling has shown me that people with an inability to trust are usually those who experienced serious privation, abuse or cruelty in their early developmental years. This is no reason to despair, however, for when we have faith in Jesus Christ we become children of God – we have a new parent and a new parentage. And He enables us to overcome whatever difficulties there may have been in our past.

PRAYER

Father, may my focus not be on what has been but on what can be, and on what will be when I am rightly related to You. Please help me grow up spiritually. In Jesus' name I ask it. Amen.

DAY 13
How to forgive
FOR READING & MEDITATION – PROVERBS 30:21–33

²¹ The earth trembles under three things;
it cannot bear up under four:
²² a servant when he becomes king,
a fool when he is stuffed with food,
²³ an unloved woman when she marries,
and a serving girl when she ousts her lady.
²⁴ Four things on earth are small,
yet they are extremely wise:
²⁵ the ants are not a strong people,
yet they store up their food in the summer;
²⁶ hyraxes are not a mighty people,
yet they make their homes in the cliffs;
²⁷ locusts have no king,
yet all of them march in ranks;
²⁸ a lizard can be caught in your hands,
yet it lives in kings' palaces.
²⁹ Three things are stately in their stride,
even four are stately in their walk:
³⁰ a lion, which is mightiest among beasts
and doesn't retreat before anything,
³¹ a strutting rooster, a goat,
and a king at the head of his army.
³² If you have been foolish by exalting yourself,
or if you've been scheming,
put your hand over your mouth.

³³ **For the churning of milk produces butter,**
and twisting a nose draws blood,
and stirring up anger produces strife.

IF, AS WE said yesterday, difficulties concerning basic trust which occur on a natural, human level can hinder our ability to trust at a spiritual level, how do we overcome this problem? The first thing we must do is demonstrate a willingness to forgive those who deprived us, hurt us or betrayed us. 'That's hard,' you might say, and my reply is this: 'Yes, particularly if you have been badly let down or abused, it is indeed hard – hard, but not impossible.'

Here's how you go about it. You focus first on how much you have been forgiven. One of the keys to forgiving others is to enter into a realised awareness of how much God has forgiven you. When people have told me during a counselling session, 'My problem is that I can't forgive,' I have usually responded by saying, 'No, that's not your problem. Your problem is that you don't know how much you have been forgiven.' It may be difficult for some to see this, especially those who have experienced betrayal and gone through deep hurt, but nothing others have done to us is as awful as what we have done to God.

If you have difficulty with that last statement it is because you do not understand the true nature of sin. Sin is taking the Creator of the universe and relegating Him to irrelevance; it is saying to the One who made us, 'I can run my life on my own terms.' Sin is insanity – and you and I have been guilty of that. Yet, because Jesus Christ died on the cross for our sins, God has forgiven us, pardoned us, and bestowed upon us His royal favour. Having been given such forgiveness can we, dare we, withhold it from anyone who has hurt us or betrayed our trust, no matter how awful or painful that hurt has been?

PRAYER

Father, Your Word is frank and open; help me to respond to it in the same way. Take from me every trace of hesitancy, every fear and apprehension, every refusal to accept responsibility. In Jesus' name I pray. Amen.

My way – or God's way

FOR READING & MEDITATION – PROVERBS 14:1–13

¹ Every wise woman builds her house,
  but a foolish one tears it down with her own hands.
² Whoever lives with integrity fears the LORD,
  but the one who is devious in his ways despises Him.
³ The proud speech of a fool [brings] a rod [of discipline],
  but the lips of the wise protect them.
⁴ Where there are no oxen, the feeding-trough is empty,
  but an abundant harvest [comes]
  through the strength of an ox.
⁵ An honest witness does not deceive,
  but a dishonest witness utters lies.
⁶ A mocker seeks wisdom and doesn't find it,
  but knowledge [comes] easily to the perceptive.
⁷ Stay away from a foolish man;
  you will gain no knowledge from his speech.
⁸ The sensible man's wisdom is to consider his way,
  but the stupidity of fools deceives [them].
⁹ Fools mock at making restitution,
  but there is goodwill among the upright.
¹⁰ The heart knows its own bitterness,
  and no outsider shares in its joy.
¹¹ The house of the wicked will be destroyed,
  but the tent of the upright will stand.

¹² **There is a way that seems right to a man,**
  but its end is the way to death.

¹³ Even in laughter a heart may be sad,
  and joy may end in grief.

TODAY WE CONTINUE looking at the steps we need to take in order to rid ourselves of the things that hinder our ability to trust. Forgiveness, we said yesterday, is the first step – but what is the second? It is the recognition of the fact that, having been let down by others, we have determined in our hearts that we will never trust another person again.

The determination never to trust another person again may be a human reaction, but it is not God's way. So many times I have heard people say, 'I can trust God but I can't trust other people.' But the Christian faith is all about relating to people. The essence of reality is passionate, other-centred relationships, as is evidenced by the perfect relationships of the Trinity – God the Father, God the Son and God the Holy Spirit. If we draw back from others because we are afraid of being betrayed then what we are in reality saying is this: 'I can't trust God enough to hold me when others let me down.' Those, therefore, who say, 'I can trust God but I can't trust people', are not making sense. It is more honest to say, 'I can't trust God and I can't trust people.' What we can say, if we really believe the truths of the New Testament and are willing to give ourselves to them, is this: 'I can trust God to hold me when I relate to others, irrespective of whether I am accepted or rejected.'

The determination to stay safe and self-protected is evidence that our trust is not what it should be. We must therefore bring this self-protective determination to preserve our own soul before God in an act of repentance, and indicate by an act of resolve that no matter how others may treat us, we will confidently place our trust in Him.

PRAYER

O Father, I must ask myself: Can I trust You enough to hold me when others do not come through for me? The determination to stay safe seems so right, yet it is so wrong. I turn from my way to Your way. Hold me secure. In Jesus' name. Amen.

DAY 15

Is trust idealistic?

FOR READING & MEDITATION – PROVERBS 29:19–27

¹⁹ A servant cannot be disciplined by words;
though he understands, he doesn't respond.
²⁰ Do you see a man who speaks too soon?
There is more hope for a fool than for him.
²¹ A slave pampered from his youth
will become arrogant later on.
²² An angry man stirs up conflict,
and a hot-tempered man increases rebellion.
²³ A person's pride will humble him,
but a humble spirit will gain honor.
²⁴ To be a thief's partner is to hate oneself;
he hears the curse but will not testify.
²⁵ **The fear of man is a snare,**
but the one who trusts in the LORD is protected.
²⁶ Many seek a ruler's favor,
but a man receives justice from the LORD.
²⁷ An unjust man is detestable to the righteous,
and one whose way is upright
is detestable to the wicked.

THE TRUTHS I have been putting before you in the past few days are extremely challenging – especially for those who have been badly let down or betrayed. Sometimes people have said to me, 'Isn't it idealistic to expect me to be vulnerable to further hurt after I have been let down and betrayed?' My answer is to point them to Jesus. If He can do it then so can we – providing we depend on His strength and not ours. Jesus knows better than anyone what it means to be let down and betrayed. In all the heaped-up pain of His passion, few things would have hurt Him more than being betrayed by His disciples. Take Peter's betrayal, for example (see Matt. 26:69–75). Did our Lord's experience of Peter's denial cause Him to conclude, 'Never again will I trust that man'?

Come with me to Galilee and let us see. Simon Peter, no doubt feeling disappointed and disillusioned, returns to his trade as a fisherman, whereupon Jesus pursues him and puts Himself in a position of being hurt once again. He says to Peter, '... do you love Me ...?', using the strong Greek word for love – *agapao*. Peter responds, 'Yes, Lord, You know that I love You' (John 21:15–16). Jesus opened Himself up to Peter despite the hurt He would still have been feeling from Peter's earlier betrayal *and* despite the possibility of further rejection. Jesus' openness with Peter opened up again the possibility of relationship and also opened up the way for Peter to enter into an important new role within the fledgling Church.

Jesus did not allow the hurt He felt to deter Him from continuing, even pursuing, the relationship. *That's* what I mean by vulnerability. *That's* what I mean by love.

PRAYER

Father, is it possible that You can make me so secure that I, too, am able to be vulnerable in my relationships? I must believe it; I do believe it. Help me to demonstrate it in every relationship I am called by You to pursue. In Jesus' name. Amen.

DAY 16
'Yours trustingly'
FOR READING & MEDITATION – PROVERBS 11:25–31

²⁵ A generous person will be enriched,
and the one who gives a drink of water
will receive water.

²⁶ People will curse anyone who hoards grain,
but a blessing will come to the one who sells it.

²⁷ The one who searches for what is good finds favor,
but if someone looks for trouble, it will come to him.

²⁸ **Anyone trusting in his riches will fall,**
but the righteous will flourish like foliage.

²⁹ The one who brings ruin on his household
will inherit the wind,
and a fool will be a slave
to someone whose heart is wise.

³⁰ The fruit of the righteous is a tree of life,
but violence takes lives.

³¹ If the righteous will be repaid on earth,
how much more the wicked and sinful.

WE SPEND ONE more day meditating on the important issue of trust. What have we been saying? We have concluded that trust is an essential ingredient in our relationships – both human and divine. The reason we can demonstrate trust in all our earthly relationships is because we recognise that there is One who is guiding and governing our lives, One in whom we can place our fullest confidence. We can give ourselves to others knowing that even though they let us down He will hold us in His arms and not allow us to be destroyed.

Take careful note of what I say here because many people hold God to promises He never made and are then disappointed when He doesn't do what they believed He had promised He would do. God does not promise to keep us from being hurt in our relationships, but He does promise to keep us from being destroyed.

The more you trust in God, the more effective you will be in your relationships with others. Because your ultimate trust is in God you will be free from unconscious manipulative or exploitative techniques and, drawing your security from Him, you can give yourself more freely to others. 'Love does not begin,' someone has said, 'until you expect nothing in return.' When your trust is wholly and fully in the Lord Jesus you can love like that.

If you have never done so before, decide now to put in God's hands all the hurts, traumas and betrayals of the past. Forgive all those who have let you down. Lift up your head and look into the face of the One who will never betray you. Give Him all your trust. And, I say again, keep in mind the fact that trust is not only an essential attitude in life, it is also the first step in wisdom. The wise are those who trust in God.

PRAYER

O God, break down any last barrier that may be hindering me from putting my trust fully in You. I would have the doors of my spirit turn out, not in. Help me begin and end every day by saying, 'Yours trustingly'. In Jesus' name. Amen.

DAY 17
Integrity – 'profound wisdom'
FOR READING & MEDITATION – PROVERBS 10:9–17

> 9 The one who lives with integrity lives securely,
> but whoever perverts his ways will be found out.

10 A sly wink of the eye causes grief,
and foolish lips will be destroyed.

11 The mouth of the righteous is a fountain of life,
but the mouth of the wicked conceals violence.

12 Hatred stirs up conflicts,
but love covers all offenses.

13 Wisdom is found on the lips of the discerning,
but a rod is for the back of the one who lacks sense.

14 The wise store up knowledge,
but the mouth of the fool hastens destruction.

15 A rich man's wealth is his fortified city;
the poverty of the poor is their destruction.

16 The labor of the righteous leads to life;
the activity of the wicked leads to sin.

17 The one who follows instruction is on the path to life,
but the one who rejects correction goes astray.

WE MOVE ON now to look at what I consider to be the second aspect of wisdom – *integrity*. This theme, like trust, is one that is continually emphasised in Proverbs for, as we shall see, no one can be truly successful in life without integrity.

What is integrity? The dictionary definition puts it like this: 'wholeness, soundness, trustworthiness, uprightness, honesty.' You can see at once that integrity is a moral quality, and morality is an essential characteristic of wisdom. One of the mistakes many people make when thinking about wisdom is to confuse it with learning, intelligence, brilliance or cleverness. How many times do we read in the newspaper of those who have climbed the ladder of success, have been highly educated, or have achieved great prominence in the world, only to then come tumbling down because of some issue of personal or corporate integrity?

Many professional people have a great deal of knowledge but lack wisdom. For example, you see this in the marriage counsellor who, in spite of all his credentials, can't hold his own marriage together; in the psychiatrist who, overcome by her own problems, slides into depression; in the economist who goes bankrupt playing the stock market; in the church leader who causes chaos and hurt when he leaves his family for another woman. Learning, understanding, intelligence and professional training are important – please don't hear me demean them – but if we are to be experts in the art of living, as Proverbs sets out to teach us to be, then we must see that without wisdom the things I have listed don't count for much at all.

'The simplicity of integrity is the profundity of wisdom,' says Paul Larsen. How true! How very true!

PRAYER

O God, give me in addition to trust a high degree of integrity. I want not only to trust others but I want them to trust me. You know my need and also my desire. Grant me these facets of wisdom. In Jesus' name I ask it. Amen.

DAY 18
'I would rather be right …'
FOR READING & MEDITATION – PROVERBS 8:1–11

1 Doesn't Wisdom call out?
  Doesn't Understanding make her voice heard?
2 At the heights overlooking the road,
  at the crossroads, she takes her stand.
3 Beside the gates at the entry to the city,
  at the main entrance, she cries out:
4 "People, I call out to you;
  my cry is to mankind.
5 Learn to be shrewd, you who are inexperienced;
  develop common sense, you who are foolish.
6 Listen, for I speak of noble things,
  and what my lips say is right.
7 For my mouth tells the truth,
  and wickedness is detestable to my lips.
8 All the words of my mouth are righteous;
  none of them are deceptive or perverse.
9 All of them are clear to the perceptive,
  and right to those who discover knowledge.
10 Accept my instruction instead of silver,
  and knowledge rather than pure gold.
11 **For wisdom is better than precious stones,**
  and nothing desirable can compare with it.

TODAY WE CONTINUE with the thought that another aspect of wisdom is integrity. Both we and the universe are made for truth and integrity, and both the world and we are alien to untruth and dishonesty. The universe is made for the same thing that we are made for – righteousness.

The same moral law that God has revealed in Scripture He has also stamped on human nature. He has, in fact, written His law twice – once in the text of the Bible and once in the texture of human nature; once on stone tablets and once on human hearts. The moral law is not an alien system that is unnatural for people to obey; it fits perfectly, as a hand to a glove, because it is the law of our own created being. There is a fundamental correspondence between God's law in the Bible and the one written on our hearts. We can discover our true humanness by obeying it.

Charles Spurgeon wrote to the then Prime Minister of Britain, William Gladstone, in these words: 'You do not know how those of us regard you who feel it a joy to live when a Prime Minister believes in righteousness. We believe in no man's infallibility but it is restful to be sure of one man's integrity.' What makes us so suspicious of politicians, even though politics can be a noble profession, is not that they might make mistakes, but that sometimes staying in office is more important to them than honour and candour. Henry Clay, when about to introduce to the American Congress a bill that was heavily weighted in favour of morality, was told, 'If you do this, it will kill your chances of becoming president.' His reply was, 'I would rather be right than be president.' I can almost see King Solomon's head nodding in favour of that attitude.

PRAYER

Tender and skilful Invader of my soul, I yield myself to You for the inrush of divine life that brings with it wisdom. Father, I see that the reason I am not wiser is that I do not have enough of You. Please fill me with Your Spirit. Amen.

DAY 19
'A lie has short legs'
FOR READING & MEDITATION – PROVERBS 28:18–28

¹⁸ **The one who lives with integrity will be helped,
but one who distorts right and wrong
will suddenly fall.**

¹⁹ The one who works his land
will have plenty of food,
but whoever chases fantasies
will have his fill of poverty.

²⁰ A faithful man will have many blessings,
but one in a hurry to get rich
will not go unpunished.

²¹ It is not good to show partiality—
yet a man may sin for a piece of bread.

²² A greedy man is in a hurry for wealth;
he doesn't know that poverty will come to him.

²³ One who rebukes a person will later find more favor
than one who flatters with his tongue.

²⁴ The one who robs his father or mother
and says, "That's no sin,"
is a companion to a man who destroys.

²⁵ A greedy person provokes conflict,
but whoever trusts in the LORD will prosper.

²⁶ The one who trusts in himself is a fool,
but one who walks in wisdom will be safe.

²⁷ The one who gives to the poor
will not be in need,
but one who turns his eyes away
will receive many curses.

²⁸ When the wicked come to power,
people hide,
but when they are destroyed,
the righteous flourish.

YESTERDAY WE SAID that both we and the universe are made for integrity. Let's take that thought a stage further by asking: Will the universe sustain a lie? I have no hesitation in saying that it will not, for I believe that the universe is not built for the success of a lie. The Tamils in South India have a saying that goes like this: 'The life of the cleverest lie is only eight days.' A lie may not break itself upon the universe today or tomorrow, but one day it will.

Before World War II the Germans used to say, 'Lies have short legs', meaning that they were bad in the long run. During the war that saying was changed to 'Lies have one short leg'. Why? Because Goebbels, the propaganda minister, had one short leg!

In a moral universe nobody gets away with anything. Dr Cynddylan Jones, a famous Welsh preacher, claimed, 'The worst thing about doing wrong is to be the one who does the wrong.' I don't know about you, but I used to think the text 'Be sure that your sin will find you out' (Num. 32:23, NIV) meant 'Be sure your sin will be found out'. The verse doesn't say that, though. It says your sin will find *you* out. It will register in you and demean you. We may be free to choose, but we are not free to choose the consequences of our choosing.

Any philosophy or ideology that dismisses the moral universe and tries to establish its own ideas about what is right and wrong is doomed to fall. This is what brought about the downfall of the great empires of Assyria, Greece and Rome. '... there is nothing covered that won't be uncovered' (Matt. 10:26). We either work with the moral universe and gain benefits or we work against it and face the consequences. It is as simple as that.

PRAYER

Gracious and loving Father, I see that You have designed a moral universe and that those who run against it go against the grain. Help me to be a person of integrity and truth, and thus get results, not consequences. In Jesus' name. Amen.

Can a lie be justified?

FOR READING & MEDITATION – PROVERBS 19:1–9

¹ Better a poor man who walks in integrity
than someone who has deceitful lips and is a fool.

² Even zeal is not good without knowledge,
and the one who acts hastily sins.

³ A man's own foolishness leads him astray,
yet his heart rages against the LORD.

⁴ Wealth attracts many friends,
but a poor man is separated from his friend.

⁵ A false witness will not go unpunished,
and one who utters lies will not escape.

⁶ Many seek the favor of a ruler,
and everyone is a friend of one who gives gifts.

⁷ All the brothers of a poor man hate him;
how much more do his friends
keep their distance from him!
He may pursue [them with] words,
[but] they are not [there].

⁸ The one who acquires good sense loves himself;
one who safeguards understanding finds success.

⁹ **A false witness will not go unpunished,
and one who utters lies perishes.**

WE CONTINUE LOOKING at the question we raised yesterday: Will the universe sustain a lie? Contemporary society is increasingly facing and needing to deal with 'situational ethics', which would have us believe that sometimes, under certain situations, a lie is admissible. I think that is a dangerous and deadly path. A lie is never right – no matter what attempts we might make to justify it. 'God is not a man who lies', we are told in Numbers 23:19, and in 1 John 2:21 we read, '… no lie comes from the truth'. God Himself cannot lie, and He will never delegate to you the task of lying for Him. When we weave lies and dishonesties into the tapestry of our lives we actually weave fire into our very being – here and hereafter: '… all liars shall have their part in the lake which burns with fire and brimstone' (Rev. 21:8, NKJV).

Situational ethics often proposes possible scenarios to justify a position, such as, 'What if someone came to your house to murder a member of your family and asked if that person was in. Would it not be right to lie in those circumstances?' Can you see the thrust of this question? It is the argument, 'This is what we must and ought to do because it makes sense'. But once we view sin as a 'must' and as an 'ought' it is magically turned into something that is 'good'.

The Bible does not advise that anyone, in any situation, *ought* to sin. 1 Corinthians 10:13 teaches that because God is faithful, we will never find ourselves in a situation where we *must* sin, and promises that there will always be a way of escape. God never puts us in such a situation or calls upon us to break one of His laws in order to keep another of His commands.

PRAYER

O Father, in a world that seems to be always looking for excuses and exceptions, help me to steer my life by the clear statements of Your revealed will. I want to conform to the rules – Your rules. In Jesus' name. Amen.

Two important facts

FOR READING & MEDITATION – PROVERBS 6:12–19

¹² A worthless person, a wicked man,
who goes around speaking dishonestly,
¹³ who winks his eyes, signals with his feet,
and gestures with his fingers,
¹⁴ who plots evil with perversity in his heart—
he stirs up trouble constantly.
¹⁵ Therefore calamity will strike him suddenly;
he will be shattered instantly—beyond recovery.

¹⁶ **Six things the L**ORD **hates;**
in fact, seven are detestable to Him:

¹⁷ arrogant eyes, a lying tongue,
hands that shed innocent blood,
¹⁸ a heart that plots wicked schemes,
feet eager to run to evil,

¹⁹ **a lying witness who gives false testimony,**
and one who stirs up trouble among brothers.

WE RETURN TO the question we started to consider yesterday: What if someone came to your house to murder a member of your family and asked if that person was in – how would you respond? Would it not be right to lie in such circumstances? Situational ethics may demand a 'Yes'. The Bible, in my opinion, says, 'No'.

Situational ethics is notorious for putting forward hypothetical situations in which a person *must* sin because that is what *ought* to be done. But when we view sin as a 'must' and an 'ought' we are finished. A Christian view of ethics rejects every constructed situation which situational ethics advances if it fails to take into account two important biblical facts. First,

God's sovereignty. God will always prepare a way out for His people. God is still alive today. Second, *the Holy Spirit's power.* The believer is encouraged not to worry about what he or she has to say in difficult situations. Jesus has promised, 'For you will be given what to say at that hour, because you are not speaking, but the Spirit of your Father is speaking through you' (Matt. 10:19–20). Also, we are told, 'Trust in the LORD with all your heart, and do not rely on your own understanding' (Prov. 3:5).

God is not ignorant or stupid. He did not fail to see that sometimes His laws would seem to contradict one another. He knew full well that there would be occasions when it might appear prudent from a human point of view to ignore one of His principles – hence His promise to us in 1 Corinthians 10:13. Those who try to excuse the breaking of any of God's moral laws on the pretext that it feels 'right' or seems 'good' sow the seeds of disruption in their own inner being. It is not the way of wisdom.

PRAYER

Father, forgive us that so often we prefer human wisdom to divine wisdom simply because it 'feels' right. Help us to trust Your Word even when it runs counter to our own feelings. In Jesus' name we pray. Amen.

Dishonesty is doomed

FOR READING & MEDITATION – PROVERBS 14:1–13

¹ Every wise woman builds her house,
but a foolish one tears it down with her own hands.

² Whoever lives with integrity fears the LORD,
but the one who is devious in his ways despises Him.

³ The proud speech of a fool [brings] a rod [of discipline],
but the lips of the wise protect them.

⁴ Where there are no oxen, the feeding-trough is empty,
but an abundant harvest [comes]
through the strength of an ox.

⁵ **An honest witness does not deceive,**
but a dishonest witness utters lies.

⁶ A mocker seeks wisdom and doesn't find it,
but knowledge [comes] easily to the perceptive.

⁷ Stay away from a foolish man;
you will gain no knowledge from his speech.

⁸ The sensible man's wisdom is to consider his way,
but the stupidity of fools deceives [them].

⁹ Fools mock at making restitution,
but there is goodwill among the upright.

¹⁰ The heart knows its own bitterness,
and no outsider shares in its joy.

¹¹ The house of the wicked will be destroyed,
but the tent of the upright will stand.

¹² There is a way that seems right to a man,
but its end is the way to death.

¹³ Even in laughter a heart may be sad,
and joy may end in grief.

WE NEED TO fix it as an axiom in our thinking that nobody gets away with anything, anywhere, any time, if that 'any thing' is dishonest or untrue. The whole history of the human race is a commentary on this. The first lie uttered by Satan was 'No! You will not die' (Gen. 3:4). And he keeps repeating that well-worn but discredited lie to every man and woman who comes into this world.

Something dies the moment you are dishonest or fail to be a person of integrity. Self-respect dies within you. Degeneration begins to damage your heart the moment dishonesty enters it. You are not so much punished for your sin as by your sin. You are punished *by* sin *for* sin. In one sense, sin is its own punishment.

The first time I was in Madras, India, I had a meal with a family who told me the story of their milkman. He had to drive his cow and calf from door to door in the hot sun and milk the cow in the presence of each housewife. 'What a clumsy way of delivering milk,' I commented. 'Ah,' said my host, 'but you see, he was discovered putting water in the milk and now, because he can't be trusted, he has to milk the cow before the eyes of everyone he serves.' The milkman's dishonesty doomed him to drudgery. The moral universe had the last word.

'Dishonesty puts sand in the machinery of life,' says one writer. I would add, 'And honesty and integrity puts oil into it.' We can choose to live with either sand or oil in our inner mechanism. I cannot say whether or not I would ever lie. I would like to think not – but I have to acknowledge I am fallible and human. However, I know this: my moral joints will creak if I am dishonest. I am made for integrity and I will not function well without it.

PRAYER

O Father, help me grasp this simple but important fact – that I am designed for truth and honesty. When I work with truth, I go leaping into life. When I work without it, I limp. Drive this truth deep into my being, I pray. Amen.

DAY 23
Truth is truth is truth
FOR READING & MEDITATION – PROVERBS 30:1–9

¹ The words of Agur son of Jakeh. The oracle.
The man's oration to Ithiel, to Ithiel and Ucal:
² I am the least intelligent of men,
and I lack man's ability to understand.
³ I have not gained wisdom,
and I have no knowledge of the Holy One.
⁴ Who has gone up to heaven and come down?
Who has gathered the wind in His hands?
Who has bound up the waters in a cloak?
Who has established all the ends of the earth?
What is His name,
and what is the name of His Son—
if you know?
⁵ Every word of God is pure;
He is a shield to those who take refuge in Him.
⁶ Don't add to His words,
or He will rebuke you, and you will be proved a liar.
⁷ Two things I ask of You;
don't deny them to me before I die:

⁸ **Keep falsehood and deceitful words far from me.**

Give me neither poverty nor wealth;

feed me with the food I need.

⁹ Otherwise, I might have too much
and deny You, saying, "Who is the LORD?"
or I might have nothing and steal,
profaning the name of my God.

INCREASINGLY, IN OUR society, integrity is in short supply. Some time ago I asked a successful businessman, 'What would you say is the greatest need in your sphere of business?' He thought for a moment, looked me straight in the eye, and said, 'Integrity.' When I asked him why, he explained, 'Almost daily I am faced with dishonesty and duplicity, and whenever I confront it people take the view that dishonesty is only a problem when it is found out.' It's interesting, however, that those who laugh at dishonesty become deeply upset when they are the victims of it.

The following statement is one that I once caught sight of in one of my grandson's books: 'An honest fisherman is a pretty uninteresting person.' Another statement made in the book was this: 'There are two things essential if you are to succeed in business – integrity and sagacity. Integrity is keeping your word and sagacity is never giving your word.' Is it any wonder that we find the thought of no moral absolutes so appealing? It is only fair to say, though, that despite the present-day trend away from honesty and integrity, there are still millions of people who would not claim to be Christians but who, nevertheless, see it as their duty to be honest, upright and decent. May their tribe increase!

Christians who lack integrity hinder the progress of the gospel in this world and set Christ's message in a false light. Determine to be honest in thought and speech and act. Lay this down as a cornerstone of your life, especially you who are young, and begin building from there. Whatever you do, shun like a plague the temptations of situational ethics and admit no exceptions. Truth is truth is truth.

PRAYER

O God, You who are the Designer of the great design, help me mould my life by it and be fully surrendered to its purposes. If I run from truth I run from myself, for I am made for truth. Keep me true, dear Lord. In Jesus' name. Amen.

Self-exploratory surgery

FOR READING & MEDITATION – PROVERBS 23:15–25

¹⁵ My son, if your heart is wise,
my heart will indeed rejoice.
¹⁶ My innermost being will cheer
when your lips say what is right.
¹⁷ Don't be jealous of sinners;
instead, always fear the LORD.
¹⁸ For then you will have a future,
and your hope will never fade.
¹⁹ Listen, my son, and be wise;
keep your mind on the right course.
²⁰ Don't associate with those who drink too much wine,
or with those who gorge themselves on meat.
²¹ For the drunkard and the glutton will become poor,
and grogginess will clothe [them] in rags.
²² Listen to your father who gave you life,
and don't despise your mother when she is old.

²³ **Buy—and do not sell—truth,
wisdom, instruction, and understanding.**

²⁴ The father of a righteous son will rejoice greatly,
and one who fathers a wise son will delight in him.
²⁵ Let your father and mother have joy,
and let her who gave birth to you rejoice.

WE SPEND ONE more day meditating on the importance of integrity. In one of his books, Charles Swindoll tells how many years ago in New York a doctor by the name of Evan O'Neil became convinced that most major operations could be performed while patients were under a local anaesthetic, thereby avoiding the risks of general anaesthesia. On 15 February 1921 he operated on himself and removed his appendix while under a local anaesthetic. The operation was a success, and it was said that he recovered faster than usually expected of patients who were given general anaesthesia.

Today I invite you to undertake some self-exploratory surgery of the soul. While fully conscious and fully aware, allow the Holy Spirit to assist you by handing you the only instrument you need for soul surgery – the infection-free scalpel of Scripture. 'For the word of God is living and effective and sharper than any two-edged sword, penetrating as far as to divide soul, spirit, joints, and marrow; it is a judge of the ideas and thoughts of the heart' (Heb. 4:12).

This is not just an interesting idea, it is something we are required to do because Scripture commands it: 'But let a man examine himself' (1 Cor. 11:28, NKJV). Right now, in God's presence, ask yourself: Am I honest? Am I a person of integrity? Can my word be trusted? Remember, only you can perform this surgery on your soul – only you. No one else but you knows the truth about yourself. You can rationalise and twist the facts and no one will know the difference – except you. And remember, too, that there can be no wisdom without morality, no expertise in living without truth and honesty. The wise are those who have integrity.

PRAYER

Father, I realise that when truth is not present in me there is as much pain as with a diseased appendix. By Your Word, and through Your Spirit, right now cut away in me all that is untrue and dishonest. For Jesus' sake. Amen.

Take another path

FOR READING & MEDITATION – PROVERBS 5:1–14

¹ My son, pay attention to my wisdom;
   listen closely to my understanding
² so that [you] may maintain discretion
   and your lips safeguard knowledge.
³ Though the lips of the forbidden woman drip honey
   and her words are smoother than oil,
⁴ in the end she's as bitter as wormwood
   and as sharp as a double-edged sword.
⁵ Her feet go down to death;
   her steps head straight for Sheol.
⁶ She doesn't consider the path of life;
   she doesn't know that her ways are unstable.
⁷ So now, [my] sons, listen to me,
   and don't turn away from the words of my mouth.

⁸ **Keep your way far from her.**

   Don't go near the door of her house.

⁹ Otherwise, you will give up your vitality to others
   and your years to someone cruel;
¹⁰ strangers will drain your resources,
   and your earnings will end up in a foreigner's house.
¹¹ At the end of your life, you will lament
   when your physical body has been consumed,
¹² and you will say, "How I hated discipline,
   and how my heart despised correction.
¹³ I didn't obey my teachers
   or listen closely to my mentors.
¹⁴ I was on the verge of complete ruin
   before the entire community."

FOLLOWING ON FROM integrity, we look now at what I believe to be the third aspect of wisdom – *personal purity*. This, too, is a major theme in Proverbs, for throughout the book we come across statements that encourage us to be chaste, virtuous, self-disciplined and pure in our relationships, especially with the opposite sex.

First, I would like to deal with the subject of chastity, as Proverbs speaks particularly to this. We live in an age that largely ignores the biblical teaching that enjoins us to keep sexual intercourse until marriage. Some sections of the Church now accept 'the new morality' which says that sexual relationships outside marriage are fine providing they are conducted in a loving and a non-manipulative relationship. I have no hesitation in rejecting this, both as not biblical and anti-relationship. The passage we have read today describes most clearly the destiny of sexual relationships outside marriage. They are fundamentally destructive.

The second half of the chapter is given over to a description of how fulfilling sexual relations can be within marriage. The emphasis of Proverbs at this point is to avoid putting yourself in a position of temptation – to keep well away from the danger of seduction. The words 'Keep to a path far from her' mean, 'Keep your distance from such a woman' (*The Message*), in other words 'Avoid an immoral woman as you would avoid a plague.'

A man once went to the great American preacher D.L. Moody with a tale of personal moral disaster and said, 'Now, Mr Moody, what would you have done if you had got into such a situation?' Moody replied, 'Man, I would never have got into it.' That's more than just common sense – that's wisdom!

PRAYER

O God, help me to help myself. Please show me how to avoid circumstances that make a fall almost inevitable. For I cannot ask You to help me out of situations unless I help myself not to get into them. Amen.

DAY 26
Don't go on his ground
FOR READING & MEDITATION – PROVERBS 4:10–27

¹⁰ Listen, my son. Accept my words,
and you will live many years.

¹¹ I am teaching you the way of wisdom;
I am guiding you on straight paths.

¹² When you walk, your steps will not be hindered;
when you run, you will not stumble.

¹³ Hold on to instruction; don't let go.
Guard it, for it is your life.

¹⁴ Don't set foot on the path of the wicked;
don't proceed in the way of evil ones.

¹⁵ Avoid it; don't travel on it.
Turn away from it, and pass it by.

¹⁶ For they can't sleep
unless they have done what is evil;
they are robbed of sleep unless they make someone stumble.

¹⁷ They eat the bread of wickedness
and drink the wine of violence.

¹⁸ The path of the righteous is like the light of dawn,
shining brighter and brighter until midday.

¹⁹ But the way of the wicked is like the darkest gloom;
they don't know what makes them stumble.

²⁰ My son, pay attention to my words;
listen closely to my sayings.

²¹ Don't lose sight of them;
keep them within your heart.

²² For they are life to those who find them,
and health to one's whole body.

²³ Guard your heart above all else,
for it is the source of life.

²⁴ Don't let your mouth speak dishonestly,
and don't let your lips talk deviously.

²⁵ **Let your eyes look forward;**
fix your gaze straight ahead.

²⁶ Carefully consider the path for your feet,
and all your ways will be established.
²⁷ Don't turn to the right or to the left;
keep your feet away from evil.

WE CONTINUE LOOKING at the issue of sexual experience and the need for it to be kept within marriage. If every man and woman were to accept and put into practice the principle of not allowing themselves to get into difficult situations where great strain is placed on physical intimacy, it would make a world of difference to the matter of temptation.

Some temptations cannot be avoided; some, however, can. Anatole France has an apocryphal story in which God and the devil are talking of a beautiful young girl. God asks, 'How dare you tempt such a lovely creature as that?' The devil replies, 'Well, she came on to my ground.'

R.W. Everrood tells another story. A young man seeking his fortune was travelling across a desert when he came across an oasis where a beautiful young girl sat spinning on a loom. Thirsty, he asked for a drink, and she responded, 'Certainly, providing you let me put these threads around you that I am spinning.' He agreed, thinking he could easily brush away the thin gossamer threads as one would brush away a spider's web. After drinking the water he fell asleep, and awoke to find himself tied by thick, strong cords. And what was more, the beautiful young girl had changed into a repulsive and ugly hag.

The best strategy with temptation is not to go near it. Paul's advice to young Timothy was 'run from these things' (1 Tim. 6:11). John Ruskin says, 'No one can honestly ask to be delivered from temptation unless he has honestly and firmly determined to do the best he can to keep out of it.' My advice to every unmarried man and woman reading these lines – and married people, too – is this: Keep out of the devil's territory. Don't go on to his ground.

PRAYER

O God, make me alert to the dangers that beset my path, and if I do move towards them unsuspectingly, grant that warning bells may ring in my heart. I know You will do Your part; help me do mine. In Jesus' name I ask it. Amen.

Take it on faith!

FOR READING & MEDITATION – PROVERBS 6:16–26

¹⁶ Six things the LORD hates;
in fact, seven are detestable to Him:
¹⁷ arrogant eyes, a lying tongue,
hands that shed innocent blood,
¹⁸ a heart that plots wicked schemes,
feet eager to run to evil,
¹⁹ a lying witness who gives false testimony,
and one who stirs up trouble among brothers.

²⁰ **My son, keep your father's command,**
and don't reject your mother's teaching.
²¹ Always bind them to your heart;
tie them around your neck.
²² When you walk here and there, they will guide you;
when you lie down, they will watch over you;
when you wake up, they will talk to you.
²³ For a commandment is a lamp, teaching is a light,
and corrective instructions are the way to life.
²⁴ They will protect you from an evil woman,
from the flattering tongue of a stranger.
²⁵ Don't lust in your heart for her beauty
or let her captivate you with her eyelashes.
²⁶ For a prostitute's fee is only a loaf of bread,
but an adulteress goes after [your] very life.

THE REAL TRUTH about sex and sexual satisfaction is difficult to fully understand outside of marriage. Many young people say to me, 'Why all these negatives in the Bible concerning sex before marriage? What is the point of all these dos and don'ts, all these prohibitions? Isn't sex a beautiful thing?'

This is what I say to them: 'Once you are married you will begin to see why there are so many negatives; it is so that you may better enjoy the positives. God doesn't give His prohibitions because sex is a bad thing; they are there to protect us from engaging in a good and beautiful thing in the wrong context. Within marriage, sexual activity is the doing of the right thing in the right place. It is only when you are married that you begin to see the purpose of all the dos and don'ts spelled out in the Bible.'

Christians are, or should be, people who take God on trust. There's not much point in confessing to be a follower of Jesus Christ if you don't believe what He tells you in His Word and instead change it to suit your convenience. Passion has always been a problem, but wisdom and passion must be properly related. You must recognise the necessity of learning to wait, which is one of the first evidences that you are growing in maturity. A young child desires immediate gratification and will cry and howl until he gets what he wants. When that child grows older and becomes more mature then the desire for gratification is brought under control. The concept of deferred satisfaction is a vital one for every young person to grasp for without it there can be no real maturity. You must learn to deny yourself now so that in the future you may experience the right thing in the right way.

PRAYER

Father, take me by the hand lest I succumb to the temptation of immediate satisfaction. If I get off the track here I will find myself in a jungle that gets more and more tangled every moment. Please guide me and hold me. Amen.

Prepare!

FOR READING & MEDITATION – PROVERBS 6:1–11

¹ My son, if you have put up security for your neighbor
or entered into an agreement with a stranger,
² you have been trapped by the words of your lips —
ensnared by the words of your mouth.
³ Do this, then, my son, and free yourself,
for you have put yourself in your neighbor's power:
Go, humble yourself, and plead with your neighbor.
⁴ Don't give sleep to your eyes
or slumber to your eyelids.
⁵ Escape like a gazelle from a hunter,
like a bird from a fowler's trap.

⁶ **Go to the ant, you slacker!**
Observe its ways and become wise.

⁷ Without leader, administrator, or ruler,
⁸ it prepares its provisions in summer;
it gathers its food during harvest.
⁹ How long will you stay in bed, you slacker?
When will you get up from your sleep?
¹⁰ A little sleep, a little slumber,
a little folding of the arms to rest,
¹¹ and your poverty will come like a robber,
your need, like a bandit.

WE CONTINUE LOOKING at the important principle of deferred satisfaction. As is apparent from verses 6 to 8 of today's reading, this is evident even in the insect world. The harvester ant doesn't spend all its time eating. Instead it runs back and forth carrying food into the nest so that it may survive the winter when there will be no food.

This picture of the ant is one that you should keep continually in your mind. It is an image included in the Word of God in order to bring instruction to the heart. Prepare for the future in every way you can, not only by denying yourself the things that God puts out of bounds, but also by giving yourself to the things you need to know to increase your effectiveness in your chosen profession or vocation. Whatever you plan to do in the days ahead of you – prepare for it. Prepare by study and also by prayer.

The wisdom of learning to wait and preparing for the future applies to everyone regardless of age. Whenever you have to do anything, whatever it might be – either public or private – prepare for it. This may require you to put something else off for the time being so that you can give yourself to the task in hand. There are no short cuts to success. I prepared myself for years by filling my heart and mind with the Word of God, and then, when the time came, God called me to launch these Bible notes that you are now reading. Frequently people have asked, 'How can you continue to write year after year after year?' I know it would not have been possible had I not, many years ago, denied myself many things so that I could prepare.

Whatever God asks you to do, don't take His blessing for granted – *prepare.*

PRAYER

Father, Your knife cuts deep but Your cuts are always redemptive. Forgive me for taking so much for granted and for not giving myself to the tasks to which You have called me. Help me to be a prepared person. In Jesus' name I ask it. Amen.

Giving all to God

FOR READING & MEDITATION – PROVERBS 8:1–11

¹ Doesn't Wisdom call out?
Doesn't Understanding make her voice heard?
² At the heights overlooking the road,
at the crossroads, she takes her stand.
³ Beside the gates at the entry to the city,
at the main entrance, she cries out:
⁴ "People, I call out to you;
my cry is to mankind.
⁵ Learn to be shrewd, you who are inexperienced;
develop common sense, you who are foolish.
⁶ Listen, for I speak of noble things,
and what my lips say is right.
⁷ For my mouth tells the truth,
and wickedness is detestable to my lips.
⁸ All the words of my mouth are righteous;
none of them are deceptive or perverse.
⁹ All of them are clear to the perceptive,
and right to those who discover knowledge.

¹⁰ **Accept my instruction instead of silver,**
and knowledge rather than pure gold.

¹¹ For wisdom is better than precious stones,
and nothing desirable can compare with it.

PEOPLE WHO STRUGGLE with this concept of deferred satisfaction, in other words, learning to wait, ought to take another look at the contestants who prepare for sports events – especially the Olympic Games. You see men and women pushing themselves almost beyond endurance in order to gain a prize for themselves, their club or their country. I don't think that all the training is unmitigated pleasure. Indeed, I know it isn't. The rigorous regime involves going through the pain barrier. So why are they doing it? They are demonstrating the principle of deferred satisfaction. They are willing to endure suffering now in order to win in the future. The pressure, the denial of legitimate pleasures, the strong self-discipline, the tough training, are all outweighed by the hope of winning.

You see, the idea of deferred satisfaction is not a uniquely Christian idea. It has been recognised by reflective people throughout more than 2,000 years of history. Plato talks about it, and so does Socrates. Greek philosophy talks about the control of the passions by self-discipline and encourages the development of virtue by self-denial.

The Christian message teaches us that God came to this world in the Person of His Son in order to set up a rescue mission to save us from an everlasting hell. If we believe that Jesus is God's Son we are saved, but not that we might sit back and indulge ourselves in the thought. We are saved to serve. If non-Christians can deny themselves present satisfaction for future gains and go to such lengths to win a prize, how much more ought we, who serve the risen Christ? Dare we stand by and watch them do for gold what we are not prepared to do for God?

PRAYER

Father, Your school is strict but the end is redemption. Your instructions, however hard and uncompromising, are ultimately my salvation. Help me to see the end from the beginning and to use all my powers in reaching for the goal. Amen.

Sin breaks God's heart

FOR READING & MEDITATION – PROVERBS 6:27–35

27 Can a man embrace fire
and his clothes not be burned?
28 Can a man walk on coals
without scorching his feet?
29 So it is with the one who sleeps with
another man's wife;
no one who touches her will go unpunished.
30 People don't despise the thief if he steals
to satisfy himself when he is hungry.
31 Still, if caught, he must pay seven times as much;
he must give up all the wealth in his house.

32 **The one who commits adultery lacks sense;**
whoever does so destroys himself.

33 He will get a beating and dishonor,
and his disgrace will never be removed.
34 For jealousy enrages a husband,
and he will show no mercy when he takes revenge.
35 He will not be appeased by anything
or be persuaded by lavish gifts.

WE HAVE TALKED about chastity; let's talk now about faithfulness. Chastity is purity prior to marriage; faithfulness is virtue within marriage. Love cannot be love unless it includes faithfulness, and God wants everyone who enters into marriage to be loyal and true. When we say that God is love (1 John 4:8), we are also saying that God is faithful because, I repeat, love cannot be love unless faithfulness is an integral part of it.

Marriage is a covenant. Many people argue, 'It's just a piece of paper and fifteen minutes of a couple's time.' But hold on a minute. If you understand that life is fundamentally based on relationships, that the only ethical relationship is love, and that love is faithfulness, then the covenant of marriage is the most precious thing in life. Both in the Old and New Testaments a theme that appears constantly is the covenant aspect of love. We read, 'He is a faithful God, keeping his covenant of love ...' (Deut. 7:9, NIV). And when you study the covenants of Scripture you will find this: that God keeps His covenants even though they are broken by the other side. The relationship between Jehovah and Israel is often pictured as the relationship between a husband and wife. Israel becomes the wayward, unfaithful wife who commits adultery. But God is still faithful to His covenant. God says, 'I will never break My covenant. You can count on it. I am God.'

People may shy away from commitment in a relationship, claiming they want to be 'free' – but without commitment is it really love? Love is a commitment, and when men and women indulge in sex before marriage or a so-called affair they don't just break God's laws; they also break His heart.

PRAYER

O Father, in an age when anything goes, may I be an exhibition to the world around of what it means to be a follower of You. Help me to keep all my relationships pure. For Your dear name's sake. Amen.

Be a person of passion

FOR READING & MEDITATION – PROVERBS 29:1–18

¹ One who becomes stiff-necked,
   after many reprimands
   will be broken suddenly—
   and without a remedy.
² When the righteous flourish, the people rejoice,
   but when the wicked rule, people groan.
³ A man who loves wisdom brings joy to his father,
   but one who consorts with prostitutes destroys his wealth.
⁴ By justice a king brings stability to a land,
   but a man [who demands] "contributions"
   demolishes it.
⁵ A man who flatters his neighbor
   spreads a net for his feet.
⁶ An evil man is caught by sin,
   but the righteous one sings and rejoices.
⁷ The righteous person knows the rights of the poor,
   but the wicked one does not understand these concerns.
⁸ Mockers inflame a city,
   but the wise turn away anger.
⁹ If a wise man goes to court with a fool,
   there will be ranting and raving but no resolution.
¹⁰ Bloodthirsty men hate an honest person,
    but the upright care about him.
¹¹ A fool gives full vent to his anger,
    but a wise man holds it in check.
¹² If a ruler listens to lies,
    all his servants will be wicked.
¹³ The poor and the oppressor have this in common:
    the LORD gives light to the eyes of both.
¹⁴ A king who judges the poor with fairness—
    his throne will be established forever.
¹⁵ A rod of correction imparts wisdom,
    but a youth left to himself
    is a disgrace to his mother.

¹⁶ When the wicked increase, rebellion increases,
   but the righteous will see their downfall.
¹⁷ Discipline your son, and he will give you comfort;
   he will also give you delight.

¹⁸ **Without revelation people run wild,
   but one who keeps the law will be happy.**

OVER THE PAST few days we have been talking about the subject of passion – the romantic passion of a man or a woman. Prior to marriage the passion has to be managed, and within marriage it is focused on one's partner – and on one's partner alone.

But how do we keep passion moving along the right lines? Do you remember the story of Odysseus in Greek mythology? He sailed with his crew past an island inhabited by the Sirens – creatures who had the bodies of birds, the heads of women and very beautiful voices. When the Sirens began to sing, passing sailors were so entranced that they sailed towards the island, only to be dashed to pieces and destroyed on the jagged rocks. So Odysseus asked Orpheus, the greatest harpist in the ancient world, to play for him as they sailed past the island, and the music he created was far more beautiful than that provided by the Sirens. One passion overwhelmed the other.

What every one of us needs in our lives is a passion so powerful that it transcends all other passions. In God we find that passion. When our lives are touched by Him and we drink from His life-giving stream, our hearts are filled with a passion that keeps every other passion under control. Is not this what happened to Joseph? When Potiphar's wife tried to seduce him he fled from the house crying, 'So how could I do such a great evil and sin against God?' (Gen. 39:9). His passion for God overwhelmed all other passions.

When Christ, who is the wisdom of God and the power of God, is allowed to live at the centre of our lives then His passion keeps every other passion where it ought to be – under control.

PRAYER

O Christ, come into my being afresh this day and light the fire of passion for You that will bring every other passion in my life under its complete control. This I ask for the honour and glory of Your precious name. Amen.

DAY 32

'Honeysuckle Christians'

FOR READING & MEDITATION – PROVERBS 11:25–31

²⁵ **A generous person will be enriched,**
and the one who gives a drink of water
will receive water.

²⁶ People will curse anyone who hoards grain,
but a blessing will come to the one who sells it.

²⁷ The one who searches for what is good finds favor,
but if someone looks for trouble, it will come to him.

²⁸ Anyone trusting in his riches will fall,
but the righteous will flourish like foliage.

²⁹ The one who brings ruin on his household
will inherit the wind,
and a fool will be a slave
to someone whose heart is wise.

³⁰ The fruit of the righteous is a tree of life,
but violence takes lives.

³¹ If the righteous will be repaid on earth,
how much more the wicked and sinful.

WE COME NOW to what I consider to be a fourth aspect of wisdom – *generosity*. This subject, too, is a favourite theme of the book of Proverbs. Our text for today tells us that when we move out of ourselves and give to others, we ourselves are refreshed. An old Welsh proverb says, 'The greatest joy in giving is to be the one who gives.'

Now, we must not take today's text to mean that we ought to focus on generosity because it brings rewards. Generosity that is exercised simply for the purpose of reward is not true generosity. The reward simply comes as a by-product of giving. I have heard ethicists – those who study questions of right and wrong – pull today's text to pieces. They say that this, and similar statements found in the Word of God, make Christianity a form of sophisticated selfishness. Christians, they claim, give to others because it makes them feel good, not because it is the right thing to do or the right way to live. Christianity, they conclude, is an indirect form of selfishness. Well, we must admit that some Christians may look at things in this way but I imagine they are few and far between.

I love the way in which Charles Harthern, a preacher of a different generation, described giving: 'Some give like a sponge – only when they are squeezed. Some give like Moses' rock – only when they are hit. True Christians, however, give like the honeysuckle – because they delight to give.' That's the secret – giving because we delight to give. The generous hand comes from a generous heart. If the heart is not generous then, however much the hand gives, there is no true generosity.

PRAYER

Gracious and loving heavenly Father, I ask for the blessing not only of trust, integrity and personal purity, but of generosity also. And I ask not just to get a blessing but to give a blessing. In Jesus' name I pray. Amen.

DAY 33
Divine mathematics
FOR READING & MEDITATION – PROVERBS 11:16–24

¹⁶ A gracious woman gains honor,
    but violent men gain [only] riches.
¹⁷ A kind man benefits himself,
    but a cruel man brings disaster on himself.
¹⁸ The wicked man earns an empty wage,
    but the one who sows righteousness, a true reward.
¹⁹ Genuine righteousness [leads] to life,
    but pursuing evil [leads] to death.
²⁰ Those with twisted minds are detestable to the LORD,
    but those with blameless conduct are His delight.
²¹ Be assured that the wicked
    will not go unpunished,
    but the offspring of the righteous will escape.
²² A beautiful woman who rejects good sense
    is like a gold ring in a pig's snout.
²³ The desire of the righteous [turns out] well,
    but the hope of the wicked [leads to] wrath.

²⁴ **One person gives freely,**

    yet gains more;

    another withholds what is right,

    only to become poor.

WE CONTINUE TO meditate on the wisdom of generosity. What all the passages in the book of Proverbs that talk about generosity really reveal is that selfishness short-circuits human happiness and that the route to joy is liberality — liberality with our talents, our treasure and our time.

Today's text is, of course, difficult for some to accept because it violates all the rules of mathematics. How can it be that the more you give away the more you have, and the less you give the poorer you become? It doesn't seem logical! Well, let Lord Bertrand Russell, one of the greatest mathematicians of the twentieth century, comment on that: 'Mathematics and logic have nothing to do with reality.' David Rivett, an accountant and former director of CWR, said that in working with the ministry he found that God has a quite different arithmetic from that to which he, as an accountant, is accustomed. For example – what do five and two make? Seven? Yes, in man's arithmetic, but not in God's. In God's arithmetic five and two make five – thousand. How come, I hear you say? Well, five loaves and two fish – the little lunch which a boy once gave to Jesus – were taken by Him and turned into enough food to feed five thousand (see John 6:1– 13). And just to add to the point – 12 baskets of leftovers were gathered up by the disciples after everyone had eaten their fill!

Nature, we are told, abhors a vacuum; it is the same in the spiritual realm. Liberality and generosity create a vacuum into which God flows, enabling us to give and to go on giving. I cannot explain it, but I have witnessed it countless times. Over the decades I have seen it happen again and again and again.

PRAYER

O God, You who are always reaching out to me in generosity and love, help me this day to do the same. Grant that I may quicken and awaken some life by the generosity that comes from my life. For Your own dear name's sake. Amen.

DAY 34
'Giving with a warm hand'
FOR READING & MEDITATION – PROVERBS 22:1–9

¹ A good name is to be chosen over great wealth;
   favor is better than silver and gold.
² The rich and the poor have this in common:
   the LORD made them both.
³ A sensible person sees danger and takes cover,
   but the inexperienced keep going and are punished.
⁴ The result of humility is fear of the LORD,
   along with wealth, honor, and life.
⁵ There are thorns and snares on the path of the crooked;
   the one who guards himself stays far from them.
⁶ Teach a youth about the way he should go;
   even when he is old he will not depart from it.
⁷ The rich rule over the poor,
   and the borrower is a slave to the lender.
⁸ The one who sows injustice will reap disaster,
   and the rod of his fury will be destroyed.
⁹ **A generous person will be blessed,**
   for he shares his food with the poor.

TODO: TODAY WE ASK the question: Does being a generous person
mean you will always have plenty of money or material goods to give away?
Not necessarily. This would be a naïve interpretation of the principle we
are discussing. No text should be taken in isolation. Verses of Scripture
must be put into context if we are to get a more complete picture of the
truth under discussion. Some Christians cannot be trusted with large
amounts of money or lots of earthly goods; they just would not know how
to manage them.

That said, we should note that you do not have to be rich in order to be
generous. A pauper can give like a prince, providing he or she has the right

spirit. An old Jewish saying puts it like this: 'The man who gives with a smile gives more than the man who gives with a frown.' It is the *spirit* of generosity that the Bible focuses on first of all – the spirit that gives, not because it wants to get something in return, but because it simply delights to give. One person has defined generosity as 'giving with a warm hand'. I like that. Who likes to receive anything from a cold hand?

As you know, the opposite of generosity is selfishness, and just as generosity is a facet of wisdom so selfishness is a facet of foolishness. A teacher once said to a class, 'Unselfishness means voluntarily going without something you need. Can anyone give me an example?' A little boy raised his hand and said, 'Yes, sometimes I go without a bath even though I need one.' We smile, but how many of us do something very similar by turning a truth on its head to take the pressure off ourselves?

'The love of liberty,' said William Hazlitt, 'is the love of others. The love of power is the love of ourselves.'

PRAYER

O God, help me to be a person who gives 'with a warm hand'. Melt any coldness and iciness there may be in my spirit and please make me a magnanimous and generous person. Fire me with a passion to give. In Jesus' name I ask it. Amen.

DAY 35

The generous eye

FOR READING & MEDITATION – PROVERBS 28:18–28

¹⁸ The one who lives with integrity will be helped,
but one who distorts right and wrong
will suddenly fall.

¹⁹ The one who works his land
will have plenty of food,
but whoever chases fantasies
will have his fill of poverty.

²⁰ A faithful man will have many blessings,
but one in a hurry to get rich
will not go unpunished.

²¹ It is not good to show partiality—
yet a man may sin for a piece of bread.

²² A greedy man is in a hurry for wealth;
he doesn't know that poverty will come to him.

²³ One who rebukes a person will later find more favor
than one who flatters with his tongue.

²⁴ The one who robs his father or mother
and says, "That's no sin,"
is a companion to a man who destroys.

²⁵ A greedy person provokes conflict,
but whoever trusts in the LORD will prosper.

²⁶ The one who trusts in himself is a fool,
but one who walks in wisdom will be safe.

²⁷ **The one who gives to the poor**
will not be in need,
but one who turns his eyes away
will receive many curses.

²⁸ When the wicked come to power,
people hide,
but when they are destroyed,
the righteous flourish.

WE CONTINUE MEDITATING on the subject of generosity. Not only the book of Proverbs but the whole Bible has a great deal to say on this subject. Jesus made a powerful statement, recorded in Matthew 6:22, which in the Moffatt translation reads: '... if your Eye is generous, the whole of your body will be illumined.' 'If your Eye ...' These words indicate that if your whole outlook on life, your whole way of looking at things, is generous then your whole personality is filled with light.

Jesus was generous towards all – the poor, the outcasts of society, the sinful, the unlovely – and His whole personality was full of light. When we are in touch with Jesus, the fount of all wisdom, then He generates that same generosity within us. We begin to see everyone and everything with the same generous eye.

It is generosity that is at the heart of all good relationships. On occasions I have had the privilege of visiting Sweden and Norway, and I used to wonder why it is that the Swedes and the Norwegians have such a brotherly attitude towards each other. They seem to have an unbreakable bond that ties them as one people. Then I discovered that in 1905, when Norway wanted to break free from Swedish control, the Swedish people responded by recognising Norwegian independence. The Swedes responded according to the Christian ethos of the ruling family who were in power at that time, and King Oscar II renounced his claim to the Norwegian throne. This generosity in giving freedom without war or bitterness created a basic soundness that now flavours all their contacts with one another.

The generous eye fills the whole body of relationships with light. Generosity, like love, never fails.

PRAYER

Lord Jesus, Your generous eye saw in me things I could never see in myself. Help me this day to make generosity the basis of all my dealings with everyone. May Your generosity generate generosity in me. In Jesus' name I pray. Amen.

Suppose … just suppose …

FOR READING & MEDITATION – PROVERBS 3:13–35

¹³ Happy is a man who finds wisdom
  and who acquires understanding,
¹⁴ for she is more profitable than silver,
  and her revenue is better than gold.
¹⁵ She is more precious than jewels;
  nothing you desire compares with her.
¹⁶ Long life is in her right hand;
  in her left, riches and honor.
¹⁷ Her ways are pleasant,
  and all her paths, peaceful.
¹⁸ She is a tree of life to those who embrace her,
  and those who hold on to her are happy.
¹⁹ The LORD founded the earth by wisdom
  and established the heavens by understanding.
²⁰ By His knowledge the watery depths broke open,
  and the clouds dripped with dew.
²¹ Maintain [your] competence and discretion.
  My son, don't lose sight of them.
²² They will be life for you
  and adornment for your neck.
²³ Then you will go safely on your way;
  your foot will not stumble.
²⁴ When you lie down, you will not be afraid;
  you will lie down, and your sleep will be pleasant.
²⁵ Don't fear sudden danger
  or the ruin of the wicked when it comes,
²⁶ for the LORD will be your confidence
  and will keep your foot from a snare.

²⁷ When it is in your power,
  don't withhold good from the one to whom it is due.
²⁸ **Don't say to your neighbor, "Go away! Come back later.**
  I'll give it tomorrow"—when it is there with you.

29 Don't plan any harm against your neighbor,
   for he trusts you and lives near you.
30 Don't accuse anyone without cause,
   when he has done you no harm.
31 Don't envy a violent man
   or choose any of his ways;
32 for the devious are detestable to the LORD,
   but He is a friend to the upright.
33 The LORD's curse is on the household of the wicked,
   but He blesses the home of the righteous;
34 He mocks those who mock,
   but gives grace to the humble.
35 The wise will inherit honor,
   but He holds up fools to dishonor.

THROUGHOUT THE BIBLE we find the truth that the generous generate generosity in others. When Ananias, a potential victim of Saul's spite and rage, put his hands on the blinded zealot and generously said, 'Brother Saul' (Acts 9:17), that generosity, I believe, touched something deep within the newly converted disciple. It helped to start the greatest Christian missionary of the centuries on his way.

Suppose, just suppose, the little boy who gave his loaves and fishes to Jesus (John 6:9) had said to himself, 'This meal is mine and I won't share it with anyone.' If he had done that he would not have witnessed one of the most amazing miracles of all time. And suppose, also, that the disciples, instead of serving the multiplied bread and fishes to the crowd, had decided to pile it high in one place and make a charge for it in order to boost their funds. What do you think would have happened? I doubt if we would ever have heard of them again. They would have sunk into obscurity.

And again, suppose the man who owned the colt on which Jesus rode into Jerusalem (Matt. 21:1–3) had said, 'This colt is mine and I will not let it go to anyone else.' What would have happened? For the rest of his days he would have had an inner debate over whether or not he was justified in keeping it for himself.

I have no doubt that today, and certainly in the immediate future, we will come across opportunities to be generous. If we fail to respond to these opportunities, who knows what rivers will never flow, what great ministries will never be initiated, what mighty things will not get done? God has opened His doors and been generous to us; let us not fail to open up our doors and be generous to others.

PRAYER

O Father, may I be the channel and not the stopping place of all Your generosity to me. When I see how generosity has opened up such power in the life of others, I fear that I may fail. Help me, dear Father. In Jesus' name. Amen.

DAY 37

A framework for generosity

FOR READING & MEDITATION – PROVERBS 11:1–10

> ¹ Dishonest scales are detestable to the LORD,
> but an accurate weight is His delight.

² When pride comes, disgrace follows,
but with humility comes wisdom.
³ The integrity of the upright guides them,
but the perversity of the treacherous destroys them.
⁴ Wealth is not profitable on a day of wrath,
but righteousness rescues from death.
⁵ The righteousness of the blameless clears his path,
but the wicked person will fall because of his wickedness.
⁶ The righteousness of the upright rescues them,
but the treacherous are trapped by their own desires.
⁷ When the wicked dies,
his expectation comes to nothing,
and hope placed in wealth vanishes.
⁸ The righteous is rescued from trouble;
in his place, the wicked goes in.
⁹ With his mouth the ungodly destroys his neighbor,
but through knowledge the righteous are rescued.
¹⁰ When the righteous thrive, a city rejoices,
and when the wicked die, there is joyful shouting.

AS WE HAVE seen over the past few days, generosity is an important life principle, so now we ask ourselves: How do we go about establishing a framework for generosity? Here are my suggestions.

First, decide that nothing you possess is your own but that everything you have belongs to God. This puts God in His place and you in yours. You are now ready to manage His possessions, not as you like but as He likes. This is real freedom. It gives you a sense of accountability to Another – God. You get your life orders not from a whim, a notion, self-impulse or whatever takes your fancy, but from the One who saved you and redeemed you.

Second, go over your life and see what can be classed as your needs and what merely constitutes your wants. Your needs are important, and God has promised to supply them (Phil. 4:19), but what about your wants? Ah, that's another matter. You need as much as will make you fit – spiritually, physically and mentally – for the purposes of God while you are here on the earth. Beyond that, what you have belongs to the needs of others. How do you decide what can be classed as your needs? No one can decide this question for you – though they can make suggestions – for you are accountable to God. Go over your life item by item and ask Him for directions. Your family should figure prominently in your concerns, but you must check everything with the Lord.

Third, fix it as an axiom in your mind that you will be generous to people, not for the good feelings that generosity brings, but because you are determined to bless them in some way. We should never be generous in order to get a blessing; we should be generous in order to be a blessing.

PRAYER

Father, I am thankful that my life is fixed in You and from that foundation I am able to build a framework for generosity. From now on please help me to give freely and willingly. In Jesus' name I pray. Amen.

DAY 38

Completing the framework

FOR READING & MEDITATION – PROVERBS 14:27–35

27 The fear of the LORD is a fountain of life,
   turning people from the snares of death.
28 A large population is a king's splendor,
   but a shortage of people is a ruler's devastation.
29 A patient person [shows] great understanding,
   but a quick-tempered one promotes foolishness.
30 A tranquil heart is life to the body,
   but jealousy is rottenness to the bones.
31 **The one who oppresses the poor insults their Maker,**
   but one who is kind to the needy honors Him.
32 The wicked are thrown down by their own sin,
   but the righteous have a refuge when they die.
33 Wisdom resides in the heart of the discerning;
   she is known even among fools.
34 Righteousness exalts a nation,
   but sin is a disgrace to any people.
35 A king favors a wise servant,
   but his anger falls on a disgraceful one.

WE SPEND ONE more day looking at how to build a framework for generosity. My fourth suggestion is this: give at least a tenth of your earnings to God's work. The giving of a tithe is seen by many as legalistic, but the tithe is really an acknowledgement that all that we have, including the remaining nine-tenths, belongs to God. The Hebrews waved the firstfruits of the harvest before the Lord as an acknowledgement that the coming harvest belonged to Him (Lev. 23:9–11). Some will be able to give far more than a tenth of their income, but the tithe is a good place to begin.

Fifth, make your will under God's direction and maintain a balance between responsibility for your family and the continuing work of God.

Make sure your relatives don't waste what God has given you to invest in His kingdom. You might need help and advice here from a mature Christian.

Sixth, remember that the principle of generosity applies not only to your treasure but also to your talents and your time. Each day ask God to show you ways of using your talents and time for Him. I have referred before to John Wesley's advice but I believe it is worth repeating: 'Make all you can; save all you can; give all you can.'

Seventh, accept the smallest opportunity to be generous as a training ground for faithfulness. 'You were faithful over a few things; I will put you in charge of many things' (Matt. 25:21). Don't wait for the big opportunities to be generous but start with the next opportunity that comes your way – no matter how small it may be. Get ready for the larger opportunities by doing the small ones well.

Why does the Bible make so much of generosity? Because the truly generous are the truly wise.

PRAYER

Father, just like Simon Peter, who gave Your Son his boat from which to preach, I give You my treasure, my talents and my time for You to use as Your pulpit – today and every day. In Christ's name. Amen.

DAY 39

A disturbing of complacency

FOR READING & MEDITATION – PROVERBS 13:1–10

¹ A wise son [hears his] father's instruction,
but a mocker doesn't listen to rebuke.
² From the words of his mouth,
a man will enjoy good things,
but treacherous people have an appetite for violence.
³ The one who guards his mouth protects his life;
the one who opens his lips invites his own ruin.
⁴ **The slacker craves, yet has nothing,**
but the diligent is fully satisfied.
⁵ The righteous hate lying,
but the wicked act disgustingly and disgracefully.
⁶ Righteousness guards people of integrity,
but wickedness undermines the sinner.
⁷ One man pretends to be rich but has nothing;
another pretends to be poor but has great wealth.
⁸ Riches are a ransom for a man's life,
but a poor man hears no threat.
⁹ The light of the righteous shines brightly,
but the lamp of the wicked is extinguished.
¹⁰ Arrogance leads to nothing but strife,
but wisdom is gained by those who take advice.

TODAY WE COME to what I believe is the fifth of the seven aspects of wisdom – *diligence*. The wise are those who persevere, who persist in following that which is right, who stick with it and never give up. One of the great needs of our day, in my opinion, is for diligence to become an essential part of life again – particularly, some might say, among the young. A Christian educator writes, 'Diligence in the young is something that is built into them not by precept but by example. In today's world there are not enough examples of diligence to inspire or guide.' Some may consider this an exaggeration, but I think I would have to say that diligence seems no longer to be esteemed in the way it once was.

Prior to my conversion, I was greatly lacking in diligence, not from lack of encouragement or example, I hasten to add, but simply because I chose not to apply myself to anything. Then in my teens Jesus Christ came into my life, and by His coming disturbed my complacency and challenged me to apply myself to the things that needed to be done. The result? I covered more ground in the first year following my conversion than I had done in the previous two or three years. A year or so after my conversion an uncle of mine said to my father, 'I wondered whether he had been really converted but by his diligence I can see he has found God.'

Forgive the continued personal emphasis, but if it had not been for the diligence I learned at the feet of Christ I would not have been able to write *Every Day with Jesus* for over 40 years. I learned diligence from the One whose life and character were the very epitome of this quality – Jesus. He is diligence personified.

PRAYER

Gracious and loving Father, I also long for this facet of wisdom – the quality of diligence. Prune from me all inertia and indolence, all lethargy and dodging of responsibility, all complacency and pride. In Jesus' name I ask it. Amen.

DAY 40

'A second wind'

FOR READING & MEDITATION – PROVERBS 10:1–8

1. A wise son brings joy to his father,
   but a foolish son, heartache to his mother.
2. Ill-gotten gains do not profit anyone,
   but righteousness rescues from death.
3. The LORD will not let the righteous go hungry,
   but He denies the wicked what they crave.

4. **Idle hands make one poor,**
   but diligent hands bring riches.

5. The son who gathers during summer is prudent;
   the son who sleeps during harvest is disgraceful.
6. Blessings are on the head of the righteous,
   but the mouth of the wicked conceals violence.
7. The remembrance of the righteous is a blessing,
   but the name of the wicked will rot.
8. A wise heart accepts commands,
   but foolish lips will be destroyed.

YESTERDAY WE ENDED with the statement 'Jesus is diligence personified'. Here is an example of what I mean. One day the disciples said to Jesus, '"… just now the Jews tried to stone You, and You're going there again?". "Aren't there 12 hours in a day?" Jesus answered' (John 11:8–9). What was Jesus saying in this rather puzzling statement? He was saying that it is not a question of what will or will not happen. There are twelve hours in the day – enough time for what must be done – and He must get on and complete His task. What a sense of inward drive is conveyed by these words. The purpose for which He had come into the world was inwardly pressing Him forward, despite the threats and obstacles that came His way, and He would pursue the task right to the end.

It is possible, of course, to be a person of diligence without knowing Jesus Christ, but those who know Him have an added passion which motivates them and drives them forward to the completion of a task. Yesterday I said that when Christ came into my life He disturbed my complacency. Someone else sums up his experience like this: 'When Jesus came into my life He became the conscience of my conscience.' A middle-aged lady I knew who found the Lord said, 'Christ gave me a second wind in the race of life.'

I wonder, as you read these notes, are you on the point of giving up a task in which you know you are rightly engaged? Have lethargy, inertia and indifference crept in and threatened to take over your soul? Reach up and put your hand in the hand of Jesus. Talk with Him now and draw from Him the strength you need. Then in His name go out and throw yourself once again into the task.

PRAYER

Loving Father, I am thankful for all the benefits of 'common grace' but I am even more thankful for the special grace that is mine through Christ Jesus. Help me to be diligent and use that special grace to Your praise and glory. Amen.

DAY 41

Know the difference

FOR READING & MEDITATION – PROVERBS 4:10–27

¹⁰ Listen, my son. Accept my words,
and you will live many years.
¹¹ I am teaching you the way of wisdom;
I am guiding you on straight paths.
¹² When you walk, your steps will not be hindered;
when you run, you will not stumble.
¹³ Hold on to instruction; don't let go.
Guard it, for it is your life.
¹⁴ Don't set foot on the path of the wicked;
don't proceed in the way of evil ones.
¹⁵ Avoid it; don't travel on it.
Turn away from it, and pass it by.
¹⁶ For they can't sleep
unless they have done what is evil;
they are robbed of sleep unless they make someone stumble.
¹⁷ They eat the bread of wickedness
and drink the wine of violence.
¹⁸ The path of the righteous is like the light of dawn,
shining brighter and brighter until midday.
¹⁹ But the way of the wicked is like the darkest gloom;
they don't know what makes them stumble.

²⁰ My son, pay attention to my words;
listen closely to my sayings.
²¹ Don't lose sight of them;
keep them within your heart.
²² For they are life to those who find them,
and health to one's whole body.

²³ **Guard your heart above all else,**
for it is the source of life.

²⁴ Don't let your mouth speak dishonestly,
and don't let your lips talk deviously.
²⁵ Let your eyes look forward;
fix your gaze straight ahead.

26 Carefully consider the path for your feet,
and all your ways will be established.
27 Don't turn to the right or to the left;
keep your feet away from evil.

TODAY WE PAUSE to make clear the difference between diligence and obstinacy. Some people known to me have experienced spiritual shipwreck because they didn't discern the difference between these two characteristics. They thought they were being diligent when actually they were being obstinate. When asked to clarify the difference between perseverance and obstinacy, a student wrote, 'One is a strong will and the other is a strong won't.' Diligence is dogged perseverance; obstinacy is dogged inflexibility and self-will.

A certain man whose life was full of promise as far as the Christian ministry was concerned now spends his days in sadness and regret because he did not know the difference between diligence and obstinacy. He embarked on a project that he thought was God's will for him, and when things started to go wrong, instead of checking his guidance, he continued to press on and ended up in failure. He did not listen to his family, friends and those who loved him, refusing to change course, and carried on regardless. Having set himself to complete a particular task, he did not have the wisdom to realise that what he was doing was not being diligent but obstinate. The result is that he lives in perpetual disillusionment.

When Jesus came to Calvary, He said, 'I have finished the work which You [the Father] have given Me to do' (John 17:4, NKJV). Notice the word 'You'. There were many who would have liked Jesus to do this and that, to go here and go there, but He did only what the Father required Him to do. Saying 'yes' to God's will and pursuing it is diligence. Saying 'yes' to a thing that is not God's will and pursuing that is obstinacy. We had better learn the difference.

PRAYER

Father, help me differentiate between diligence and obstinacy so that at the end of my time here on earth I, too, will be able to say, 'I have finished the work which You have given me to do.' Amen.

The secret of survival

FOR READING & MEDITATION – PROVERBS 12:11–28

¹¹ The one who works his land will have plenty of food,
but whoever chases fantasies lacks sense.

¹² The wicked desire what evil men have,
but the root of the righteous produces [fruit].

¹³ An evil man is trapped by [his] rebellious speech,
but the righteous escapes from trouble.

¹⁴ A man will be satisfied with good
by the words of his mouth,
and the work of a man's hands will reward him.

¹⁵ A fool's way is right in his own eyes,
but whoever listens to counsel is wise.

¹⁶ A fool's displeasure is known at once,
but whoever ignores an insult is sensible.

¹⁷ Whoever speaks the truth declares what is right,
but a false witness, deceit.

¹⁸ There is one who speaks rashly,
like a piercing sword;
but the tongue of the wise [brings] healing.

¹⁹ Truthful lips endure forever,
but a lying tongue, only a moment.

²⁰ Deceit is in the hearts of those who plot evil,
but those who promote peace have joy.

²¹ No disaster [overcomes] the righteous,
but the wicked are full of misery.

²² Lying lips are detestable to the LORD,
but faithful people are His delight.

²³ A shrewd person conceals knowledge,
but a foolish heart publicizes stupidity.

²⁴ **The diligent hand will rule,
but laziness will lead to forced labor.**

²⁵ Anxiety in a man's heart weighs it down,
but a good word cheers it up.

²⁶ A righteous man is careful in dealing with his neighbor,
but the ways of wicked men lead them astray.

27 A lazy man doesn't roast his game,
   but to a diligent man, his wealth is precious.
28 There is life in the path of righteousness,
   but another path leads to death.

A COUPLE OF days ago I said that many people who do not know Christ advocate the value of diligence. It goes back to the subject of 'common grace' that I talked about at the beginning of these meditations. There are many people who, even though they are not Christians, catch sight of the fact that the universe is made for wisdom and that to live effectively on this earth we have to search for wisdom and cultivate it. Through rational thought and intuition these people come to the conclusion that without diligence life is more like a cage than a challenge.

Victor Frankl was one such person. Frankl, a Jew, was an Austrian neurologist and psychiatrist as well as a survivor of the Holocaust and the horror of the concentration camps. He was the founder of logotherapy and existential analysis. Sadly, his father died in the Theresienstadt ghetto; his mother, brother and wife all died in Auschwitz. Throughout his years in a concentration camp he gave himself to the task of finding out why it was that despite tremendous odds some survived while others gave up the will to live. He discovered that the reason why some people gave up was because they had no sense of meaning. Those who had a meaning or purpose to live for, such as the hope of seeing a loved one again, found it easier to keep going despite the greatest odds, while those who had no meaning or purpose simply gave up.

Frankl discovered by empirical means what another Jew discovered by revelation – that in order to persist, we need hope. That other Jew was the apostle Paul, and he showed greater understanding than Frankl when he said, 'Christ in you, the hope of glory' (Col. 1:27). Christ *with* us is one thing; Christ *in* us – now that's another.

PRAYER

O Father, how can I sufficiently thank You for the joy of having Christ within? His presence within gives me a hope that provides meaning in the deepest and darkest moments of my life. For this, Lord, I am eternally grateful. Amen.

DAY 43

So wise – yet so foolish!

FOR READING & MEDITATION – PROVERBS 2:1–11

¹ My son, if you accept my words
and store up my commands within you,

² listening closely to wisdom

and directing your heart to understanding;

³ furthermore, if you call out to insight
and lift your voice to understanding,
⁴ if you seek it like silver
and search for it like hidden treasure,

⁵ then you will understand the fear of the LORD

and discover the knowledge of God.

⁶ For the LORD gives wisdom;
from His mouth come knowledge and understanding.
⁷ He stores up success for the upright;
He is a shield for those who live with integrity
⁸ so that He may guard the paths of justice
and protect the way of His loyal followers.
⁹ Then you will understand righteousness, justice,
and integrity—every good path.
¹⁰ For wisdom will enter your mind,
and knowledge will delight your heart.
¹¹ Discretion will watch over you,
and understanding will guard you ...

WE PICK UP from where we left off yesterday when we said that in order to persist we need hope. We made the point, you remember, that having Christ *with* us is one thing; having Him *in* us is another.

Permit me to continue to explore a little more of Victor Frankl's thinking. Although he became a well-known and highly respected psychiatrist, Frankl seemed unable to accept the divine perspective. Listen to this: 'The reason so many people are unhappy is because they fail to understand what human existence is all about. Until we recognise that life is not just something to be enjoyed but rather is a task that each of us is assigned, we will never find meaning in our lives and we will never be truly happy.' So near yet so far! So wise yet so foolish! He understood that without meaning life is drab and difficult, but he failed to go on to the next step and say that true meaning can be found only in Christ. He was both a delight and a disappointment – a delight because he said, 'Life is a task', but a disappointment because he failed to recognise that we need Christ to help us perform that task.

Yes, in many ways life is a task – a tough one that is sometimes well-nigh unbearable. That's why we need to have Jesus at the centre of our lives. We then pursue the divine task with the help of divine grace. Both the writer of Proverbs and Victor Frankl said that life works better when we give ourselves to it with diligence, but there is much more to it than this. Why do you think God inspired the writer of Proverbs to personify wisdom? Because, as we saw, it prepares us to face the fact that true wisdom is not merely found in principles but in a Person. And that Person is Jesus Christ.

PRAYER

O Father, how sad when the wise of this world show themselves to be so foolish. They get so close – yet fall at the crucial moment. Thank You, Father, that through Jesus I dwell in wisdom and am indwelt by it. Amen.

DAY 44
What's the point?
FOR READING & MEDITATION – PROVERBS 21:1–15

¹ A king's heart is a water channel in the LORD's hand:
  He directs it wherever He chooses.
² All the ways of a man seem right to him,
  but the LORD evaluates the motives.
³ Doing what is righteous and just
  is more acceptable to the LORD than sacrifice.
⁴ The lamp that guides the wicked—
  haughty eyes and an arrogant heart—is sin.

**⁵ The plans of the diligent certainly lead to profit,
but anyone who is reckless only becomes poor.**

⁶ Making a fortune through a lying tongue
  is a vanishing mist, a pursuit of death.
⁷ The violence of the wicked sweeps them away
  because they refuse to act justly.
⁸ A guilty man's conduct is crooked,
  but the behavior of the innocent is upright.
⁹ Better to live on the corner of a roof
  than to share a house with a nagging wife.
¹⁰ A wicked person desires evil;
  he has no consideration for his neighbor.
¹¹ When a mocker is punished,
  the inexperienced become wiser;
  when one teaches a wise man,
  he acquires knowledge.
¹² The Righteous One considers the house of the wicked;
  He brings the wicked to ruin.
¹³ The one who shuts his ears to the cry of the poor
  will himself also call out and not be answered.
¹⁴ A secret gift soothes anger,
  and a covert bribe, fierce rage.
¹⁵ Justice executed is a joy to the righteous
  but a terror to those who practice iniquity.

TODAY WE ASK ourselves: What is the point of diligence? Why keep persevering with a task? I'll tell you why. It is because it is in the arena of perseverance that true character is forged, shaped, tempered and polished. It is in the daily grind – in the hard and often tedious duties of life – that the character of Jesus is given the maximum opportunity to be reproduced in us, replacing what Charles Swindoll calls that 'thin, fragile internal theology' with 'a tough reliable set of convictions that enable us to handle life rather than escape from it'.

Listen to what the apostle Paul says about this in Romans 5:3–4 (NIV): 'We also rejoice in our sufferings, [why?] because we know that suffering produces perseverance; perseverance, character; and character, hope.' Because life is a task, we need strength to face it, not speed to escape from it. When the foundations shake beneath our feet, when Christian friends or even leaders allow themselves to fall into immorality, when the anchor points of civilisation disappear, when the bottom of our world seems to drop out and brutal blows push us up against the ropes and pound the very life out of us, we need what diligence and perseverance offer us – willingness to face whatever comes, determination to stand firm, knowing that Jesus is not just with us but in us, insight to see Christ's hand in everything, and character enough to continue.

Without diligence, we will stumble and fall. With it, we can survive and overcome. The astute of this world are wise enough to recognise that no advances can be made in life without diligence. How much more ought we, who name the name of Christ and have Him living within us, recognise this also?

PRAYER

O God, help me see that out of the raw materials of human living I must fashion the important quality of diligence. Help me never to forget that the rewards are far greater than the cost. In Jesus' name. Amen.

The 'Four Spiritual Flaws'

FOR READING & MEDITATION – PROVERBS 20:1–13

¹ Wine is a mocker, beer is a brawler,
and whoever staggers because of them is not wise.

² A king's terrible wrath is like the roaring of a lion;
anyone who provokes him endangers himself.

³ It is honorable for a man to resolve a dispute,
but any fool can get himself into a quarrel.

⁴ **The slacker does not plow during planting season;
at harvest time he looks, and there is nothing.**

⁵ Counsel in a man's heart is deep water;
but a man of understanding draws it up.

⁶ Many a man proclaims his own loyalty,
but who can find a trustworthy man?

⁷ The one who lives with integrity is righteous;
his children who come after him will be happy.

⁸ A king sitting on a throne to judge
sifts out all evil with his eyes.

⁹ Who can say, "I have kept my heart pure;
I am cleansed from my sin"?

¹⁰ Differing weights and varying measures—
both are detestable to the LORD.

¹¹ Even a young man is known by his actions—
by whether his behavior is pure and upright.

¹² The hearing ear and the seeing eye—
the LORD made them both.

¹³ Don't love sleep, or you will become poor;
open your eyes, and you'll have enough to eat.

YESTERDAY WE SAW that diligently ploughing through life's tasks and problems produces in the end something exceedingly precious – character. Have you ever heard about the 'Four Spiritual Laws'? They have been used greatly by many evangelists, but today I would like to talk instead about the 'Four Spiritual Flaws'. These are four common misconceptions concerning the tough questions and difficult tasks of the Christian life, and unless they are nailed, diligence will have no meaning.

Flaw No. 1: Once you become a Christian, you will never have any more problems. It's not true. In fact, quite the opposite may happen – your problems may increase. What is true, however, is that Christ will be there to share your problems and get you through them.

Flaw No. 2: If you are having problems then you must be lacking in some way spiritually. A number of problems can arise because of this, but certainly not all. Some of the most godly people I know have wrestled with gigantic problems. If you have any doubt about this, read the story of Job.

Flaw No. 3: Never admit to anything being a problem; if you do, negativism will take over your life. This is complete nonsense. If you don't face a matter fairly and squarely then you will live in denial, which is, by the way, the opposite of integrity.

Flaw No. 4: All problems can be resolved by the application of the right verses of Scripture. Again, this is not so. After many years I still have unanswered questions concerning God's dealings with me, and know I might have to wait until I arrive in eternity to see things clearly. Here on earth we are big enough to ask questions but not big enough to understand the answers. Diligence must keep us going.

PRAYER

Father, I would be rid of all flawed thinking. Show me that I am not called to understand, but to stand. Give me grace to keep going even in the face of every one of life's unanswered questions. In Jesus' name I pray. Amen.

DAY 46

Diligence does pay off

FOR READING & MEDITATION – PROVERBS 24:23–34

23 These [sayings] also belong to the wise:
It is not good to show partiality in judgment.

24 Whoever says to the guilty, "You are innocent"—
people will curse him, and tribes will denounce him;

25 but it will go well with those who convict the guilty,
and a generous blessing will come to them.

26 He who gives an honest answer
gives a kiss on the lips.

27 Complete your outdoor work, and prepare your field;
afterwards, build your house.

28 Don't testify against your neighbor without cause.
Don't deceive with your lips.

29 Don't say, "I'll do to him what he did to me;
I'll repay the man for what he has done."

30 I went by the field of a slacker
and by the vineyard of a man lacking sense.

31 **Thistles had come up everywhere,**

weeds covered the ground,

and the stone wall was ruined.

32 I saw, and took it to heart;
I looked, and received instruction:

33 a little sleep, a little slumber,
a little folding of the arms to rest,

34 and your poverty will come like a robber,
your need, like a bandit.

FOR ONE MORE day we think about the subject of diligence. What are diligence and perseverance all about? They involve sticking to a task you know God wants you to do until it is completed, irrespective of the difficulties and frustrations.

Diligence does pay off. Have you heard the story of the two frogs who fell into a bucket of cream? They tried very hard to get out by climbing up the side of the bucket, but each time they slipped back again. Finally, one said, 'We'll never get out of here,' so he gave up, stopped kicking and drowned. The other frog persevered and kicked and kicked and kicked. Suddenly, he felt something hard beneath his feet and discovered that his kicking had turned the cream into butter. He hopped on top of it and was able to leap out to safety.

Someone has described diligence as 'an archaic word'. Even though it may appear diligence does not play a big part in today's world, it certainly plays a big part in the kingdom of God. Those who have done great exploits for God have been men and women of persistence and perseverance. One of the greatest examples of diligence in the Bible is the life of the apostle Paul. The verses that best illustrate this are these: 'We are pressured in every way but not crushed; we are perplexed but not in despair; we are persecuted but not abandoned; we are struck down but not destroyed' (2 Cor. 4:8–9). Paul kept going when others would have given up.

I love the story of Sir Winston Churchill who, during his last years, and though failing and feeble, stood up to address a group of university students and said, 'I have just one thing to say to you: Never give up. Never, never give up. Never, never, never give up.' He sat down to a standing ovation.

PRAYER

Father, I see that life can be made or broken at the place of continuance. Give me, I pray, this aspect of wisdom so that, like a postage stamp, I will stick to one thing until I get there. In Jesus' name I ask it. Amen.

DAY 47

The weight of words

FOR READING & MEDITATION – PROVERBS 10:9–17

⁹ The one who lives with integrity lives securely,
   but whoever perverts his ways will be found out.
¹⁰ A sly wink of the eye causes grief,
   and foolish lips will be destroyed.
¹¹ **The mouth of the righteous is a fountain of life,**
   but the mouth of the wicked conceals violence.
¹² Hatred stirs up conflicts,
   but love covers all offenses.
¹³ Wisdom is found on the lips of the discerning,
   but a rod is for the back of the one who lacks sense.
¹⁴ The wise store up knowledge,
   but the mouth of the fool hastens destruction.
¹⁵ A rich man's wealth is his fortified city;
   the poverty of the poor is their destruction.
¹⁶ The labor of the righteous leads to life;
   the activity of the wicked leads to sin.
¹⁷ The one who follows instruction is on the path to life,
   but the one who rejects correction goes astray.

WE LOOK NOW at the sixth aspect of wisdom – *watchfulness with words*. Anyone who fails to understand the importance of words and the effect they can have for good or bad is not a wise person. The book of Proverbs has a great deal to say about the power of words, and this is without doubt one of its major themes. Today's text implies that there is a transfer of wisdom from one person to another when wise words are used, but that unwise words have the opposite effect.

Whenever I have been involved in preparation for marriage or marriage counselling I have talked to couples about the weight of their words. I have given them examples of the emotional scars that can be left by bitter words.

How many adults, for example, still struggle from bitter words spoken to them when they were children – words such as 'I wish you had never been born!'? Many a man and woman have told me that a statement such as 'I'm sorry I ever married you', carries as much force as a physical blow. Words have the potential to destroy or build up, to hurt or heal, to bless or blister, to bring comfort or consternation.

Some Eastern religions teach that ultimate reality is silence. Lao-tse, the famous Chinese philosopher, said, 'The word that can be uttered is not the divine word; that word is Silence.' I believe that ultimate reality is relationship – relationship with a God who speaks. God broke the silence of eternity with the words 'Let there be light' (Gen. 1:3). Lao-tse had to say that ultimate reality was silence for he knew nothing of a God who speaks. With words, God created a world. We do the same. Our words create a world of order or disorder, of cosmos or chaos. Be wise – watch your words.

PRAYER

Father, I see that when You spoke, You created a world, and that when I speak, I do the same. Give me the wisdom to use words in a way that will build up and not pull down, construct and not destruct. This I ask in Jesus' name. Amen.

DAY 48
Words that scar
FOR READING & MEDITATION – PROVERBS 12:11–28

¹¹ The one who works his land will have plenty of food,
but whoever chases fantasies lacks sense.
¹² The wicked desire what evil men have,
but the root of the righteous produces [fruit].
¹³ An evil man is trapped by [his] rebellious speech,
but the righteous escapes from trouble.
¹⁴ A man will be satisfied with good
by the words of his mouth,
and the work of a man's hands will reward him.
¹⁵ A fool's way is right in his own eyes,
but whoever listens to counsel is wise.
¹⁶ A fool's displeasure is known at once,
but whoever ignores an insult is sensible.
¹⁷ Whoever speaks the truth declares what is right,
but a false witness, deceit.

¹⁸ **There is one who speaks rashly,**
like a piercing sword;
but the tongue of the wise [brings] healing.

¹⁹ Truthful lips endure forever,
but a lying tongue, only a moment.
²⁰ Deceit is in the hearts of those who plot evil,
but those who promote peace have joy.
²¹ No disaster [overcomes] the righteous,
but the wicked are full of misery.
²² Lying lips are detestable to the LORD,
but faithful people are His delight.
²³ A shrewd person conceals knowledge,
but a foolish heart publicizes stupidity.
²⁴ The diligent hand will rule,
but laziness will lead to forced labor.
²⁵ Anxiety in a man's heart weighs it down,
but a good word cheers it up.

²⁶ A righteous man is careful in dealing with his neighbor,
   but the ways of wicked men lead them astray.
²⁷ A lazy man doesn't roast his game,
   but to a diligent man, his wealth is precious.
²⁸ There is life in the path of righteousness,
   but another path leads to death.

DID YOU EVER say or sing these words in the school playground when you were a child: 'Sticks and stones may break my bones, but words will never hurt me'? It's not true. Words do hurt and produce emotional scars that can stay with us for life. I remember counselling a woman who could not break free from the bondage of a name her father gave her when she was a child: 'The devil's daughter.' She was freed from it eventually, but not without hours of deep counselling and intense struggle.

Unkind or cutting words are like deadly missiles that penetrate all the soul's defences and blast a hole in the personality, creating damage that may take years to repair. On the other hand, words that are encouraging can lift and cheer the soul in a way that is quite amazing. C.E. Macartney tells how, passing through the corridor of a hospital one day, he saw sitting on a bench a minister whom he had known. The man was well advanced in years and broken in health. As a result of his condition he had given up his church responsibilities, and was unable to participate in any kind of pulpit ministry. Macartney says, 'I turned to speak to him, expecting to hear from him some word of melancholy reminiscence or present gloom, but I received a pleasant surprise. He told me that a woman going by had just spoken with him and told him that a message he had given many years ago had been the means of bringing her to Christ. The glow on his face was something I shall never forget.'

How wonderful it will be if today you and I can say a cheerful and encouraging word to someone that will bless them, lighten their darkness, and minister the life of God into their soul. At least let's try!

PRAYER

O Father, may I not be like the person who looked into a mirror and then went away, forgetting what he looked like. Having looked into the mirror of Your Word I see what I should be. Please help me to be that person. In Jesus' name. Amen.

Driven personalities

FOR READING & MEDITATION – PROVERBS 18:1–24

¹ One who isolates himself pursues [selfish] desires;
he rebels against all sound judgment.

² A fool does not delight in understanding,
but only wants to show off his opinions.

³ When a wicked man comes, shame does also,
and along with dishonor, disgrace.

⁴ The words of a man's mouth are deep waters,
a flowing river, a fountain of wisdom.

⁵ It is not good to show partiality to the guilty
by perverting the justice due the innocent.

⁶ A fool's lips lead to strife,
and his mouth provokes a beating.

⁷ A fool's mouth is his devastation,
and his lips are a trap for his life.

⁸ A gossip's words are like choice food
that goes down to one's innermost being.

⁹ The one who is truly lazy in his work
is brother to a vandal.

¹⁰ The name of the LORD is a strong tower;
the righteous run to it and are protected.

¹¹ A rich man's wealth is his fortified city;
in his imagination it is like a high wall.

¹² Before his downfall a man's heart is proud,
but before honor comes humility.

¹³ The one who gives an answer before he listens—
this is foolishness and disgrace for him.

¹⁴ A man's spirit can endure sickness,
but who can survive a broken spirit?

¹⁵ The mind of the discerning acquires knowledge,
and the ear of the wise seeks it.

¹⁶ A gift opens doors for a man
and brings him before the great.

¹⁷ The first to state his case seems right
until another comes and cross-examines him.

18 [Casting] the lot ends quarrels
   and separates powerful opponents.
19 An offended brother is [harder to reach]
   than a fortified city,
   and quarrels are like the bars of a fortress.
20 From the fruit of his mouth a man's stomach is satisfied;
   he is filled with the product of his lips.
21 **Life and death are in the power of the tongue,**
   and those who love it will eat its fruit.
22 A man who finds a wife finds a good thing
   and obtains favor from the LORD.
23 The poor man pleads,
   but the rich one answers roughly.
24 A man with many friends may be harmed,
   but there is a friend who stays closer than a brother.

TODAY WE CONTINUE meditating on the awesome power of words. It is important not to think that your words will be overlooked or easily erased. Even to this day I can remember the words of a teacher who made me stand up in a crowded classroom and said something that pierced my heart, leaving a deep scar. The hurt has gone now and forgiveness has dealt with the residual effects, but the memory burned within me for years. Any counsellor will tell you that the words spoken to a child in the early years have shaped and moulded that child's life either for good or for bad.

A minister tells of talking to a 42-year-old man who was frantically working himself into a state of exhaustion – 'a volatile human being whose temper exploded at the slightest hint of disagreement or criticism'. He found that during his childhood this man's father repeatedly told him, 'You are not going to amount to anything.' Every time his father lost his temper he would repeat this statement to the boy. Thirty years later the man still bore the pain of his father's verbal malpractice and was *driven* to prove his father wrong. This is an example of what people mean when they refer to those who are *driven*. This man was *driven* by the lash of bitter and cruel words spoken to him years earlier.

Take, on the other hand, this example of another man to whom I talked some time ago. He told me that his father used to hug him every day and say, 'You are so special to me. There is no one in this world who could take your place.' That man grew up full of life and with a personality characterised by optimism. Proverbs is right: words of death destroy, words of life build up and give increasing strength.

PRAYER

Father, I would be a builder and not a destroyer of human personalities. Forgive me for the many foolish and unwise words I have spoken. From this day forward help me keep a check on my speech and use words as You would use them. Amen.

DAY 50

Healing words

FOR READING & MEDITATION – PROVERBS 15:1–15

¹ A gentle answer turns away anger,
but a harsh word stirs up wrath.

² The tongue of the wise makes knowledge attractive,
but the mouth of fools blurts out foolishness.

³ The eyes of the LORD are everywhere,
observing the wicked and the good.

**⁴ The tongue that heals is a tree of life,
but a devious tongue breaks the spirit.**

⁵ A fool despises his father's instruction,
but a person who heeds correction is sensible.

⁶ The house of the righteous has great wealth,
but trouble accompanies the income of the wicked.

⁷ The lips of the wise broadcast knowledge,
but not so the heart of fools.

⁸ The sacrifice of the wicked is detestable to the LORD,
but the prayer of the upright is His delight.

⁹ The LORD detests the way of the wicked,
but He loves the one who pursues righteousness.

¹⁰ Discipline is harsh for the one who leaves the path;
the one who hates correction will die.

¹¹ Sheol and Abaddon lie open before the LORD—
how much more, human hearts.

¹² A mocker doesn't love one who corrects him;
he will not consult the wise.

¹³ A joyful heart makes a face cheerful,
but a sad heart [produces] a broken spirit.

¹⁴ A discerning mind seeks knowledge,
but the mouth of fools feeds on foolishness.

¹⁵ All the days of the oppressed are miserable,
but a cheerful heart has a continual feast.

WE HAVE BEEN emphasising how devastating it can be to receive cruel and unkind words, and how long lasting their effect can be. Today we focus on the healing power of kind and encouraging words. When Sigmund Freud found that symptoms of emotional distress could be relieved simply by talking in certain ways to his patients, he was deeply interested and intrigued. His training in what is known as 'the medical model' had conditioned him to think of people as merely biological and chemical entities whose problems arose from physical malfunctioning.

If Freud had spent some time reading the book of Proverbs he might have been less surprised to discover that words have such a powerful impact. Most effective psychotherapy has to do with letting people talk. When people put their feelings into words it seems as if the pent-up emotion flows out through the words. I once heard of a special phone line you can ring where, after you have given your credit card number, a person will spend three minutes giving you some encouraging and heartening words. The service, I understand, is now a growing industry.

As I was preparing this page I thought hard and tried to recall the most influential and healing words anyone has ever spoken to me. While I was thinking I remembered a friend coming up to me at my wife's funeral and saying, 'You will be in my thoughts every hour of the day.' How different from the sincere and well-meaning person who said to me at the same event, 'Be brave.'

We can't change the things we said yesterday, but think of the possibilities ahead of us today and tomorrow. Don't wait another day – start now. Thank God that life, as well as death, lies in the power of the tongue.

PRAYER

Father, help me minister life through my tongue this very day.
Give me opportunities to put into action what I have heard, and
help me recognise those opportunities. I would be all You want
me to be. In Jesus' name I ask it. Amen.

The most powerful word

FOR READING & MEDITATION – PROVERBS 25:11–28

¹¹ A word spoken at the right time
is like golden apples on a silver tray.

¹² A wise correction to a receptive ear
is like a gold ring or an ornament of gold.

¹³ To those who send him, a trustworthy messenger
is like the coolness of snow on a harvest day;
he refreshes the life of his masters.

¹⁴ The man who boasts about a gift that does not exist
is like clouds and wind without rain.

¹⁵ A ruler can be persuaded through patience,
and a gentle tongue can break a bone.

¹⁶ If you find honey, eat only what you need;
otherwise, you'll get sick from it and vomit.

¹⁷ Seldom set foot in your neighbor's house;
otherwise, he'll get sick of you and hate you.

¹⁸ A man giving false testimony against his neighbor
is like a club, a sword, or a sharp arrow.

¹⁹ Trusting an unreliable person in a time of trouble
is like a rotten tooth or a faltering foot.

²⁰ Singing songs to a troubled heart
is like taking off clothing on a cold day,
or like [pouring] vinegar on soda.

²¹ If your enemy is hungry, give him food to eat,
and if he is thirsty, give him water to drink;

²² for you will heap coals on his head,
and the LORD will reward you.

²³ **The north wind produces rain,
and a backbiting tongue, angry looks.**

²⁴ Better to live on the corner of a roof
than in a house shared with a nagging wife.

²⁵ Good news from a distant land
is like cold water to a parched throat.

²⁶ A righteous person who yields to the wicked
is like a muddied spring or a polluted well.

²⁷ It is not good to eat too much honey,
  or to seek glory after glory.
²⁸ A man who does not control his temper
  is like a city whose wall is broken down.

IT'S ASTONISHING THE effect words can have upon you. This is why the writer of Proverbs returns so frequently to the matter of words and the way they ought to be used. I shall never forget sitting in London Airport one day in 1968 waiting for a flight to the USA and, to my horror, hearing an announcer say, 'The flight to New York is ready for its final departure'!

Here's a teaser I would like to drop in that highlights the way words can be used. Professor Ernest Brennick of Columbia University, USA, is credited with inventing the following sentence, which can be made to have eight different meanings by placing the word 'only' in all possible positions in it: 'I hit him in the eye yesterday.' Please don't write requesting all the permutations; work them out for yourself. Someone has compiled a list of the most powerful words in the English language: 'The bitterest word – alone. The most revered word – mother. The most feared word – death. The coldest word – no. The warmest word – friend.'

What, I wonder, is the most powerful word you have ever come across? I will tell you mine – Jesus. Charles Colson, one of President Nixon's right-hand men who, after the Watergate affair, was wonderfully converted to Christ, tells of visiting a man on death row. The man had been in a foetal position for months and would speak to no one. Charles told him the gospel and asked him to say the name Jesus. A week later he returned to find the man sitting in his chair, shaven, and the cell swept clean. When he asked what had happened, the man said, 'Jesus lives here now.' He went to the electric chair but his last words to the executioner were these: 'I'm going to be with the Lord.'

PRAYER

O Father, when I utter the name Jesus something profound happens within me. It is like an oratorio in two syllables, a library compressed into a single word. May I learn and appropriate all the power that lies behind that name. Amen.

DAY 52
A disciplined tongue
FOR READING & MEDITATION – PROVERBS 10:18–32

¹⁸ The one who conceals hatred has lying lips,
and whoever spreads slander is a fool.

**¹⁹ When there are many words, sin is unavoidable,
but the one who controls his lips is wise.**

²⁰ The tongue of the righteous is pure silver;
the heart of the wicked is of little value.

²¹ The lips of the righteous feed many,
but fools die for lack of sense.

²² The LORD's blessing enriches,
and struggle adds nothing to it.

²³ As shameful conduct is pleasure for a fool,
so wisdom is for a man of understanding.

²⁴ What the wicked dreads will come to him,
but what the righteous desires will be given to him.

²⁵ When the whirlwind passes,
the wicked are no more,
but the righteous are secure forever.

²⁶ Like vinegar to the teeth and smoke to the eyes,
so the slacker is to the one who sends him [on an errand].

²⁷ The fear of the LORD prolongs life,
but the years of the wicked are cut short.

²⁸ The hope of the righteous is joy,
but the expectation of the wicked comes to nothing.

²⁹ The way of the LORD is a stronghold for the honorable,
but destruction awaits the malicious.

³⁰ The righteous will never be shaken,
but the wicked will not remain on the earth.

³¹ The mouth of the righteous produces wisdom,
but a perverse tongue will be cut out.

³² The lips of the righteous know what is appropriate,
but the mouth of the wicked, [only] what is perverse.

I'M GLAD GOD included in the book of Proverbs the words found in our text for today as it is so easy to think that all we have to do is talk, talk, talk. It's important to talk, but talking too much is as bad as not talking at all. Sometimes a well-chosen sentence has more power than a whole paragraph. Proverbs extols rationing our words.

Once, when Thomas Edison, the inventor, was at a reception, the toastmaster stood up and complimented him on his many inventions, especially the talking machine. After the toastmaster sat down, the aged inventor rose to his feet and said, 'Thank you for those remarks, but I must correct one thing. It was God who invented the talking machine. I only invented the first one that can be shut off.'

A doctor told me that once, while writing out a prescription, he asked a woman to put out her tongue. When he had finished she said to him, 'But, doctor, you never even looked at my tongue.' The doctor replied, 'It wasn't necessary, I just wanted you to keep quiet while I wrote the prescription.' Amidst the humour of today's notes don't miss the point: words are important but don't overdo them.

I like the advice of an anonymous poet who wrote:

> If your lips would keep from slips
> Five things observe with care:
> Of whom you speak, to whom you speak,
> And how and when and where.

A wise person is someone who has a disciplined tongue. Many need to learn this for, just like the tongue in old lace-up shoes, our tongue is often the last thing to be worn out. If that is true of you ask God to help you, for an undisciplined tongue is an unloving tongue.

PRAYER

Father, I realise that often my tongue is the most difficult thing to bring under control. Yet I have the promise of Your help even in this. I give you my tongue to be bridled – please take over the reins. In Jesus' name I pray. Amen.

We become what we say

FOR READING & MEDITATION – PROVERBS 21:16–31

16 The man who strays from the way of wisdom
will come to rest
in the assembly of the departed spirits.
17 The one who loves pleasure will become a poor man;
whoever loves wine and oil will not get rich.
18 The wicked are a ransom for the righteous,
and the treacherous, for the upright.
19 Better to live in a wilderness
than with a nagging and hot-tempered wife.
20 Precious treasure and oil are in the dwelling of the wise,
but a foolish man consumes them.
21 The one who pursues righteousness and faithful love
will find life, righteousness, and honor.
22 The wise conquer a city of warriors
and bring down its mighty fortress.

23 **The one who guards his mouth and tongue**
keeps himself out of trouble.

24 The proud and arrogant person, named "Mocker,"
acts with excessive pride.
25 A slacker's craving will kill him
because his hands refuse to work.
26 He is filled with craving all day long,
but the righteous give and don't hold back.
27 The sacrifice of a wicked person is detestable—
how much more so
when he brings it with ulterior motives!
28 A lying witness will perish,
but the one who listens will speak successfully.
29 A wicked man puts on a bold face,
but the upright man considers his way.
30 No wisdom, no understanding, and no counsel
[will prevail] against the LORD.
31 A horse is prepared for the day of battle,
but victory comes from the LORD.

AT PRESENT WE are thinking about the need for a disciplined tongue. Why is this self-discipline so important? It is because the expression of a thing deepens the impression. A word uttered becomes a word made flesh – in us. We become the incarnation of what we express. When speaking to the Pharisees Jesus warned, 'By your words you will be acquitted, and by your words you will be condemned' (Matt. 12:37). After I saw that a person becomes what he says, I looked at this verse in a different light. If you tell a lie, you become a lie. Earlier, when dealing more fully with the subject of integrity, I said that the greatest punishment for telling a lie is to be the one who utters that lie. That person has to live with someone he cannot trust.

Now look at what I am saying from the opposite perspective. When we express good things, positive things, loving things, scriptural things, these things go deeper into us. How many times, when expressing something to someone, have you said to yourself, 'Because I expressed it so clearly I understand it more clearly myself.' And why? Because clear expression deepens impression. A brilliant young physicist says that he often discusses complex issues relating to physics with his wife, who doesn't know the first thing about the subject. He told a friend, 'I describe in detail what I am doing and she doesn't understand a word. But sometimes when I'm through – *I do.*'

If it is true – and I believe it is – that we become the incarnation of what we express then how careful we ought to be to ensure that what we say is guarded and governed by truth, integrity and kindness. Always remember: every word you utter becomes flesh – in you.

PRAYER

O Father, how awesome is the thought that I become the incarnation of what I express. Cleanse me deep within so that I may be pure in soul as well as speech, and honour You in all I do. Grant it please, dear Father. In Jesus' name. Amen.

DAY 54

The cause of most friction

FOR READING & MEDITATION – PROVERBS 16:21–33

21 Anyone with a wise heart is called discerning,
and pleasant speech increases learning.
22 Insight is a fountain of life for its possessor,
but folly is the instruction of fools.
23 A wise heart instructs its mouth
and increases learning with its speech.

24 **Pleasant words are a honeycomb:**

sweet to the taste and health to the body.

25 There is a way that seems right to a man,
but in the end it is the way of death.
26 A worker's appetite works for him
because his hunger urges him on.
27 A worthless man digs up evil,
and his speech is like a scorching fire.
28 A contrary man spreads conflict,
and a gossip separates friends.
29 A violent man lures his neighbor,
leading him in a way that is not good.
30 The one who narrows his eyes is planning deceptions;
the one who compresses his lips brings about evil.
31 Gray hair is a glorious crown;
it is found in the way of righteousness.
32 Patience is better than power,
and controlling one's temper, than capturing a city.
33 The lot is cast into the lap,
but its every decision is from the LORD.

NOW THAT WE have seen something of the power and importance of words, there is just one more thing I would like to add: be careful to watch your tone of voice. An old Chinese proverb says this: 'If you have a soft voice, you don't need a big stick.' I am convinced that most of the friction in human relationships is caused not so much by the words we speak as by the tone of voice in which we speak them. What we say is important, of course, but how we say it is also important. Our speech conveys our thoughts; our tone of voice, however, conveys our mood. How easy it is to say, 'I love you', in a tone that conveys the very opposite.

Proverbs does not actually say we should focus on the right tone of voice but the implication is clearly there in the command to use words that are kind and gentle and tender. Of course, you can say things in the right tone of voice without any real feelings of kindness at all. That is why the Bible urges us to do more than seek a change in behaviour, but a change that goes right down to the core of our being. Change must always come from the inside out otherwise it will not be real change. Take once again the infection-free scalpel of the Spirit – the Word of God – and, if necessary, let it cauterise your tongue. Indeed, let it go deeper – into the 'thoughts and intents of the heart' (Heb. 4:12, NKJV).

What is our conclusion after meditating these past eight days on the subject of words? Is it not this: the wise are those who understand how their words can impact another person, for good or for bad, and commit themselves to using words only as Paul instructs us in Ephesians 4:29 – words that are 'helpful for building others up' (NIV).

PRAYER

O God, I ask once more that You will help me to hold my tongue when I should and to speak when I should. My tongue can have sourness or sweetness, but it cannot have both at the same time. Give me the wisdom of a right way with words. Amen.

'A single soul in two bodies'

FOR READING & MEDITATION – PROVERBS 22:10–16

¹⁰ Drive out a mocker, and conflict goes too;
then lawsuits and dishonor will cease.

**¹¹ The one who loves a pure heart
and gracious lips—the king is his friend.**

¹² The LORD's eyes keep watch over knowledge,
but He overthrows the words of the treacherous.

¹³ The slacker says, "There's a lion outside!
I'll be killed in the streets!"

¹⁴ The mouth of the forbidden woman is a deep pit;
a man cursed by the LORD will fall into it.

¹⁵ Foolishness is tangled up in the heart of a youth;
the rod of discipline will drive it away from him.

¹⁶ Oppressing the poor to enrich oneself,
and giving to the rich—both lead only to poverty.

THE FINAL ASPECT of wisdom to occupy our attention is that of *friendship*. The wise are those who know how to make friends and remain loyal to them. The book of Proverbs emphasises the whole area of relationships – love and respect for parents, love for one's spouse, kindness to one's neighbours, and so on – but it pays particular attention to the matter of friendship. Why is friendship such an important theme in Proverbs? What exactly is friendship? And how do we go about the task of developing good friendships? These are some of the questions we must come to grips with over the next few days.

First, what exactly is friendship? Many years ago a Christian magazine offered a prize for the best definition of friendship sent in by its readers. Hundreds of definitions were received and the one that was given first prize was this: 'A friend is the one who comes in when the whole world has gone out.' My own definition of friendship is this: 'Friendship is the knitting of one soul with another so that both become stronger and better by virtue of their relationship.' I like also the definition of an ancient philosopher who said that friendship was 'a single soul dwelling in two bodies'.

The word 'friendship' is usually used in connection with non-sexual relationships between people of the same sex, but of course it can be applied equally to people of opposite sexes. It goes without saying, I think, that romantic relationships, such as courtship and marriage, should demonstrate the qualities of friendship, and it is sad when married couples live together without also being the closest of friends. If married, one's life partner ought also to be one's best friend.

PRAYER

Father, teach me the art of making friends. Help me see at the very beginning that being a friend is more important than having a friend. Save me from getting the wrong perspective on this. In Jesus' name I ask it. Amen.

The fusion of friendship

FOR READING & MEDITATION – ECCLESIASTES 4:1–12

¹Again, I observed all the acts of oppression being done under the sun. Look at the tears of those who are oppressed; they have no one to comfort them. Power is with those who oppress them; they have no one to comfort them. ²So I admired the dead, who have already died, more than the living, who are still alive. ³But better than either of them is the one who has not yet existed, who has not seen the evil activity that is done under the sun.

⁴I saw that all labor and all skillful work is due to a man's jealousy of his friend. This too is futile and a pursuit of the wind.

⁵ The fool folds his arms
   and consumes his own flesh.
⁶ Better one handful with rest,
   than two handfuls with effort and pursuit of the wind.

⁷Again, I saw futility under the sun: ⁸There is a person without a companion, without even a son or brother, and though there is no end to all his struggles, his eyes are still not content with riches. "So who am I struggling for," [he asks,] "and depriving myself from good?" This too is futile and a miserable task.

⁹Two are better than one because they have a good reward for their efforts. ¹⁰For if either falls, his companion can lift him up; but pity the one who falls without another to lift him up. ¹¹Also, if two lie down together, they can keep warm; but how can one person alone keep warm?

¹²**And if somebody overpowers one person, two can resist him. A cord of three strands is not easily broken.**

TODAY WE START to consider the question: Why is friendship so important? The reason I have turned your attention for the moment away from Proverbs and focused it on the book of Ecclesiastes (another book in the library of Wisdom Literature) is because today's reading includes verses that show us better than any other verses in the Bible the reason why friendship is so important. What they are telling us is this: it's good to have a friend because if you fall down a friend can help you up, or if you are suffering the effects of the cold a friend can help keep you warm.

It is interesting to note that to begin with the emphasis is on two people – '*two* are better than one', 'if *two* lie down' – but at the end the writer adds something very strange: 'A cord of *three* strands is not quickly broken.' Most commentaries dismiss these words as a literary device for the sake of emphasis. The NIV Study Bible, for example, describes it as 'a climactic construction'. But I believe it is much more than that; the words contain a powerful truth which it is to our disadvantage to miss or not understand.

The point being made is this: when you are in a close relationship with another person you not only have what the other person gives to you in the friendship, or you to the other person, but you have a third quality – a strength and a power which comes out of the relationship and which you could never have known had you both stayed apart. In other words, in the fusion of friendship you discover a power that could never be discovered were you not bound together in the relationship of friendship. Your strength plus your friend's strength produces a new and even greater strength.

PRAYER

Father, now I see into the heart and meaning of friendship. Out of it comes a power and a strength that is greater than the sum of the two parts. Teach me more, dear Father. In Jesus' name I ask it. Amen.

DAY 57

Synergy
FOR READING & MEDITATION – PROVERBS 17:1–17

¹ Better a dry crust with peace
than a house full of feasting with strife.

² A wise servant will rule over a disgraceful son
and share an inheritance among brothers.

³ A crucible is for silver and a smelter for gold,
but the LORD is a tester of hearts.

⁴ A wicked person listens to malicious talk;
a liar pays attention to a destructive tongue.

⁵ The one who mocks the poor insults his Maker,
and one who rejoices over disaster
will not go unpunished.

⁶ Grandchildren are the crown of the elderly,
and the pride of sons is their fathers.

⁷ Excessive speech is not appropriate on a fool's lips;
how much worse are lies for a ruler.

⁸ A bribe seems like a magic stone to its owner;
wherever he turns, he succeeds.

⁹ Whoever conceals an offense promotes love,
but whoever gossips about it separates friends.

¹⁰ A rebuke cuts into a perceptive person
more than a hundred lashes into a fool.

¹¹ An evil man seeks only rebellion;
a cruel messenger will be sent against him.

¹² Better for a man to meet a bear robbed of her cubs
than a fool in his foolishness.

¹³ If anyone returns evil for good,
evil will never depart from his house.

¹⁴ To start a conflict is to release a flood;
stop the dispute before it breaks out.

¹⁵ Acquitting the guilty and condemning the just—
both are detestable to the LORD.

¹⁶ Why does a fool have money in his hand
with no intention of buying wisdom?

> ¹⁷ **A friend loves at all times,**
> **and a brother is born for a difficult time.**

TODAY WE CONTINUE with the point we made yesterday, namely that in friendship we find the creation of a new energy that was never there before. The word that is often used to describe this is 'synergy'. The dictionary defines the word as 'the combined effect of two things that exceeds the sum of their individual effects'. It simply means that the whole is greater than the sum of its two parts.

Synergy is seen everywhere in nature. The roots of plants known as 'legumes' produce nitrogen. So if, for example, you plant beans and sweetcorn together the beans will climb up the sweetcorn and the sweetcorn will benefit from the nitrogen in the soil. When you put two pieces of wood together in a certain way they hold much more than the total of the weight held by each separately. One plus one equals three or more. Stephen Covey describes synergism in this way: '... the relationship which the parts have to each other is a part in and of itself. It is not only a part, but the most catalytic, the most empowering, the most unifying, and the most exciting part.' This is why, when understood correctly, friendship is so exciting because you don't quite know what exactly is going to happen or where it will lead. Christians, of course, who bring their friendships under the authority of God and His Word need not be concerned about anything that comes, for they have – or should have – an internal security which enables them to deal with anything and everything.

A friendship can be exhilarating, exciting and, at times, exhausting. But it can also open up new possibilities, new trails, new adventures, new territories and new continents. We live deprived lives if we live without friends.

PRAYER

Father, I see that I am made for relationships, not isolation. Help me understand this principle of synergy and how it can work to the extension of Your kingdom. This I ask in Jesus' precious and incomparable name. Amen.

'A friend with skin on'

FOR READING & MEDITATION – PROVERBS 27:17–27

¹⁷ **Iron sharpens iron,**
and one man sharpens another.

¹⁸ Whoever tends a fig tree will eat its fruit,
and whoever looks after his master will be honored.

¹⁹ As the water reflects the face,
so the heart reflects the person.

²⁰ Sheol and Abaddon are never satisfied,
and people's eyes are never satisfied.

²¹ Silver is [tested] in a crucible, gold in a smelter,
and a man, by the praise he receives.

²² Though you grind a fool
in a mortar with a pestle along with grain,
you will not separate his foolishness from him.

²³ Know well the condition of your flock,
and pay attention to your herds,

²⁴ for wealth is not forever;
not even a crown lasts for all time.

²⁵ When hay is removed and new growth appears
and the grain from the hills is gathered in,

²⁶ lambs will provide your clothing,
and goats, the price of a field;

²⁷ there will be enough goat's milk for your food—
food for your household and nourishment for your servants.

SOMETIMES I HAVE heard Christians say, 'Why do I need friends? God is my Friend – isn't that enough?' Such questions demonstrate a lack of understanding of the purpose of human relationships. Yes, God is our Friend – our closest Friend – but, as a little boy once put it, 'We need friends with skin on also.'

'To be,' said someone, 'is to be in relationships.' You won't know who you are until you are in a relationship. Paul Tillich, a well-known writer and theologian, made the same point in these words: 'You don't really know yourself until you are put over against someone other than yourself.' You see, if no one ever gives you an idea of how well or otherwise you come across, never challenges your presuppositions, never confronts you, never encourages you to open up about your problems, then parts of you remain undiscovered. Others, of course, who are not your friends can do this, but it is best done by someone who knows you well.

The other day we looked at some good definitions of friendship, but I have kept my favourite one until now as it fits in beautifully here: 'A friend is someone who knows all there is to know about you and loves you just the same.' Looking back on my life, I can see how valuable my friends have been to me. Because I have felt safe with them I have been able to reveal myself, and in the revealing I have come to know myself in a way that I could never have done with a mere acquaintance.

Yes, God is our Friend, but we need human friends also. This might be difficult for some to accept, but the more effectively we relate on a horizontal level with our human friends, the more effectively we will relate on a vertical level with our heavenly Friend.

PRAYER

Father, I see that my best friend is someone who brings out the best in me. Help me to be a best friend to someone – and to bring out the best in that person. In Jesus' name I ask it. Amen.

Steps to friendship

FOR READING & MEDITATION – PROVERBS 18:1–24

¹ One who isolates himself pursues [selfish] desires;
  he rebels against all sound judgment.
² A fool does not delight in understanding,
  but only wants to show off his opinions.
³ When a wicked man comes, shame does also,
  and along with dishonor, disgrace.
⁴ The words of a man's mouth are deep waters,
  a flowing river, a fountain of wisdom.
⁵ It is not good to show partiality to the guilty
  by perverting the justice due the innocent.
⁶ A fool's lips lead to strife,
  and his mouth provokes a beating.
⁷ A fool's mouth is his devastation,
  and his lips are a trap for his life.
⁸ A gossip's words are like choice food
  that goes down to one's innermost being.
⁹ The one who is truly lazy in his work
  is brother to a vandal.
¹⁰ The name of the LORD is a strong tower;
  the righteous run to it and are protected.
¹¹ A rich man's wealth is his fortified city;
  in his imagination it is like a high wall.
¹² Before his downfall a man's heart is proud,
  but before honor comes humility.
¹³ The one who gives an answer before he listens—
  this is foolishness and disgrace for him.
¹⁴ A man's spirit can endure sickness,
  but who can survive a broken spirit?
¹⁵ The mind of the discerning acquires knowledge,
  and the ear of the wise seeks it.
¹⁶ A gift opens doors for a man
  and brings him before the great.
¹⁷ The first to state his case seems right
  until another comes and cross-examines him.

18 [Casting] the lot ends quarrels
   and separates powerful opponents.
19 An offended brother is [harder to reach]
   than a fortified city,
   and quarrels are like the bars of a fortress.
20 From the fruit of his mouth a man's stomach is satisfied;
   he is filled with the product of his lips.
21 Life and death are in the power of the tongue,
   and those who love it will eat its fruit.
22 A man who finds a wife finds a good thing
   and obtains favor from the LORD.
23 The poor man pleads,
   but the rich one answers roughly.

24 **A man with many friends may be harmed,**
   but there is a friend who stays closer than a brother.

EVERYONE NEEDS AT least a small circle of friends – even those who are married. I feel deeply sad for anyone who does not have a friend. So today we ask ourselves: If friendship is so important, how do we go about making friends?

The first step is *be friendly*. The New King James Version of our text for today says, 'A man who has friends must himself be friendly.' You should not, however, become friendly just in order to gain a friend. This is an unhelpful motive because you are more interested in gaining a friend than being a friend. Self-centredness will get you nowhere.

Friendliness is the art of going out of yourself and appreciating others as much as you appreciate yourself. It is really a mind-set, an attitude. Dale Carnegie, in his book *How to Win Friends and Influence People* – a secular approach to the subject of friendship but full of good sense nevertheless – said, 'You can make more friends in two months by becoming interested in other people than you can in two years by trying to get other people interested in you.' The main reason why some people have no friends is because they demonstrate an unfriendly attitude. To have a friend – be one.

The second step is *allow time for friendships to develop*. In friendship it is futile to try to force doors open. Instead, be like Christ in the book of Revelation (Rev. 3:20); stand reverently at the door – and knock. Only if the door is opened from within should you go through it. Some relationships you have with people may never develop into close friendships. Don't be upset about that. If you are open and friendly then God will guide you and show you where deep friendships are to be developed.

PRAYER

Father, help me be a friend who does the knocking before I enter instead of knocking down after I have left. And show me not only how to sympathise with my friends' weaknesses, but how to draw out their strength. In Jesus' name. Amen.

DAY 60

When not a true friend

FOR READING & MEDITATION – PROVERBS 27:1–9

¹ Don't boast about tomorrow,
for you don't know what a day might bring.
² Let another praise you, and not your own mouth—
a stranger, and not your own lips.
³ A stone is heavy and sand, a burden,
but aggravation from a fool outweighs them both.
⁴ Fury is cruel, and anger is a flood,
but who can withstand jealousy?
⁵ Better an open reprimand
than concealed love.

⁶ **The wounds of a friend are trustworthy,**
but the kisses of an enemy are excessive.

⁷ A person who is full tramples on a honeycomb,
but to a hungry person, any bitter thing is sweet.
⁸ A man wandering from his home
is like a bird wandering from its nest.
⁹ Oil and incense bring joy to the heart,
and the sweetness of a friend is better than self-counsel.

WE CONTINUE LOOKING at the steps we need to take in order to win friends. The third step is *be prepared to be vulnerable*. By this I mean be prepared to be hurt. No relationship is free from pain this side of eternity – so don't expect perfection in your friendships. If your goal in life is to stay safe and comfortable then don't get involved in developing friendships. Friendships demand that you leave the comfort zone of base camp and confront an entirely new and unknown wilderness. There will be times when your words or actions are misunderstood, but stay with it when this happens. This is what friendship is all about – sticking closer than a brother. It is loving as you yourself are loved.

Fourth, *love your friend enough to talk with him or her about anything you feel is not right.* One of the greatest tests of friendship is to ask yourself: Am I prepared to lose this friendship in the interests of God's kingdom? If not, then you haven't got a true friendship. You are in it for your own reasons, not God's. You are not a true friend. Where you see wrong, deal with it, but do so lovingly, gently and firmly. You see, that's what friends are for – to help us see what we might otherwise be missing.

Fifth, *allow your friend to have other friends also.* Don't suffocate your friend by being possessive and demanding that he or she maintain just your friendship and no one else's. It is this attitude, more than any one thing, which is responsible for the death of friendships. Give your friend the freedom to move out into other relationships, to make new contacts and see new people, and be happy for them when they do so. You will desecrate a friendship if you try to dominate it.

PRAYER

O Father, may I never suffocate a friendship by being possessive. And help me to have such a secure relationship with You that I can risk losing a friend if it is in the interest of that which is right. In Jesus' name I pray. Amen.

DAY 61

No one has a double

FOR READING & MEDITATION – PROVERBS 27:10–16

> 10 **Don't abandon your friend or your father's friend,**
> **and don't go to your brother's house**
> **in your time of calamity;**
> **better a neighbor nearby than a brother far away.**

11 Be wise, my son, and bring my heart joy,
so that I can answer anyone who taunts me.
12 The sensible see danger and take cover;
the foolish keep going and are punished.
13 Take his garment,
for he has put up security for a stranger;
get collateral if it is for foreigners.
14 If one blesses his neighbor
with a loud voice early in the morning,
it will be counted as a curse to him.
15 An endless dripping on a rainy day
and a nagging wife are alike.
16 The one who controls her controls the wind
and grasps oil with his right hand.

TODAY WE CONSIDER the sixth and final step to developing friendship: *stay loyal and loving to your friends as far as you possibly can.* I say 'as far as you possibly can' because they may commit and continue in some sin, such as adultery, for example, and this demands action by the church as described in Matthew 18:15–17. Discipline may have to be given and you will need to reconsider the grounds upon which your friendship can continue. Loyalty and love in this case would mean continuing in prayer for your friend – prayer, by the way, that may take hours, not minutes.

Clearly, the matter of friendship is of major importance and those who ignore it do so at their peril. You see, the opposite of friendship is isolation.

And how much emotional damage is the result of that? 'The world is so empty,' said Goethe, the German poet and philosopher, 'if one thinks only of mountains, rivers and cities, but to know someone here and there who thinks and feels with us and, though distant, is close to us in spirit – this makes the earth an inhabited garden.'

God made us for relationships and it is His will that we cultivate a circle of friends. Every friend is different. No one has a double in friendship. The more we have, the richer we are. Dr Larry Crabb says, 'Every day we ought to move out from our base in the home and say to ourselves: Lord, help me reach out and touch someone deep in their being today, not for the rewards it brings me in terms of good feelings, but for the blessing I can be to them.'

This is the way in which Jesus lived and related to others. Perhaps this is why they called Him 'a *friend* of … sinners' (Matt. 11:19). He hated sin, but He loved the sinner.

PRAYER

Father, one thing is clear: the wise are those who know how to make friends. Guide me in my future days so that in every relationship I may be able to apply the principles I have just learned. In Jesus' name I ask it. Amen.

DAY 62
Growing in wisdom
FOR READING & MEDITATION – PROVERBS 9:10–18

¹⁰ **The fear of the LORD is the beginning of wisdom,**
and the knowledge of the Holy One is understanding.

¹¹ For by Wisdom your days will be many,
and years will be added to your life.
¹² If you are wise, you are wise for your own benefit;
if you mock, you alone will bear [the consequences]."
¹³ The woman Folly is rowdy;
she is gullible and knows nothing.
¹⁴ She sits by the doorway of her house,
on a seat at the highest point of the city,
¹⁵ calling to those who pass by,
who go straight ahead on their paths:
¹⁶ "Whoever is inexperienced, enter here!"
To the one who lacks sense, she says,
¹⁷ "Stolen water is sweet,
and bread [eaten] secretly is tasty!"
¹⁸ But he doesn't know that the departed spirits are there,
that her guests are in the depths of Sheol.

IT IS MY hope that what I set out to do at the beginning of these devotions has now been accomplished – namely, to have encouraged you to steal, drink, lie and swear as much as possible. Just in case you have forgotten, let me hasten to remind you what I mean by that statement: that from now on you will steal time out of your schedule to read continually from the book of Proverbs; that you will drink regularly from its clear refreshing waters; that you will lie on your bed at night and meditate on its great themes; and that you will swear by the grace of God to put its powerful principles into practice every day.

If you feel that I have not touched on some aspect of Proverbs then I have served you well. It will stimulate you to deeper and further study. The 'seven aspects of wisdom' I have suggested, you must remember, are the themes that I believe are the dominant ones in Proverbs. Others will have different views and different observations. Read what they have to say, too – it will help you gain even greater understanding.

My prayer is that these meditations will stimulate thousands to pursue that most glorious of all qualities – divine wisdom. But remember, do not seek wisdom for its own sake. Seek it that you might more effectively represent Jesus Christ. And beware of legalism, that soul-destroying attitude that takes greater pleasure in principles than in the Person who is behind them – our Lord Jesus Christ Himself. If you still don't know Him then bow your head this very moment, repent of every sin you have committed and quietly surrender your heart and life into His hands. Committing your way to God is the beginning of wisdom; continual trust in Him will see it develop and grow.

PRAYER

Father, please grant me this wisdom, not so that I might have an advantage over others, or to fulfil selfish needs, or even to advance my fortunes. I seek it that I might know You better, love You more, and do Your perfect will. Amen.

The book of Proverbs

1

The proverbs of Solomon
son of David, king of Israel:

2 For gaining wisdom
and being instructed;
for understanding
insightful sayings;

3 for receiving wise instruction
[in] righteousness, justice,
and integrity;

4 for teaching shrewdness
to the inexperienced,
knowledge and discretion
to a young man—

5 a wise man will listen
and increase his learning,
and a discerning man will
obtain guidance—

6 for understanding a proverb
or a parable,
the words of the wise,
and their riddles.

7 The fear of the LORD
is the beginning of knowledge;
fools despise wisdom
and instruction.

AVOID THE PATH OF THE VIOLENT

8 Listen, my son, to your father's
instruction,
and don't reject your mother's
teaching,

9 for they will be a garland of
grace on your head
and a [gold] chain around your
neck.

10 My son, if sinners entice you,
don't be persuaded.

11 If they say—"Come with us!
Let's set an ambush and kill
someone.
Let's attack some innocent
person just for fun!

12 Let's swallow them alive, like
Sheol,
still healthy as they go down to
the Pit.

13 We'll find all kinds of valuable
property
and fill our houses with
plunder.

14 Throw in your lot with us,
and we'll all share our
money"—

15 my son, don't travel that road
with them
or set foot on their path,

16 because their feet run toward
trouble
and they hurry to commit
murder.

17 It is foolish to spread a net
where any bird can see it,

18 but they set an ambush to kill
themselves;
they attack their own lives.

19 Such are the paths of all who
pursue gain dishonestly;
it takes the lives of those who
profit from it.

WISDOM'S PLEA

20 Wisdom calls out in the street;
she raises her voice in the
public squares.

21 She cries out above the
commotion;
she speaks at the entrance of
the city gates:

22 "How long, foolish ones, will
you love ignorance?
[How long] will [you] mockers

enjoy mocking
and [you] fools hate
knowledge?

23 If you turn to my discipline,
then I will pour out my spirit
on you
and teach you my words.

24 Since I called out and you
refused,
extended my hand and no one
paid attention,

25 since you neglected all my
counsel
and did not accept my
correction,

26 I, in turn, will laugh at your
calamity.
I will mock when terror strikes
you,

27 when terror strikes you like a
storm
and your calamity comes like a
whirlwind,
when trouble and stress
overcome you.

28 Then they will call me, but I
won't answer;
they will search for me, but
won't find me.

29 Because they hated knowledge,
didn't choose to fear the LORD,

30 were not interested in my
counsel,
and rejected all my correction,

31 they will eat the fruit of their way
and be glutted with their own
schemes.

32 For the waywardness of the
inexperienced will kill them,
and the complacency of fools
will destroy them.

33 But whoever listens to me will
live securely
and be free from the fear of
danger."

WISDOM'S WORTH

2 My son, if you accept my words
and store up my commands
within you,

2 listening closely to wisdom
and directing your heart to
understanding;

3 furthermore, if you call out to
insight
and lift your voice to
understanding,

4 if you seek it like silver
and search for it like hidden
treasure,

5 then you will understand the
fear of the LORD
and discover the knowledge
of God.

6 For the LORD gives wisdom;
from His mouth
come knowledge and
understanding.

7 He stores up success for the
upright;
He is a shield for those who live
with integrity

8 so that He may guard the paths
of justice
and protect the way of His
loyal followers.

9 Then you will understand
righteousness, justice,
and integrity—every good
path.

10 For wisdom will enter your
mind,

and knowledge will delight
your heart.
11 Discretion will watch over you,
and understanding will guard
you,
12 rescuing you from the way of
evil—
from the one who says perverse
things,
13 [from] those who abandon the
right paths
to walk in ways of darkness,
14 [from] those who enjoy doing
evil
and celebrate perversity,
15 whose paths are crooked,
and whose ways are devious.
16 It will rescue you from a
forbidden woman,
from a stranger with her
flattering talk,
17 who abandons the companion
of her youth
and forgets the covenant of her
God;
18 for her house sinks down to
death
and her ways to the land of the
departed spirits.
19 None return who go to her;
none reach the paths of life.
20 So follow the way of good
people,
and keep to the paths of the
righteous.
21 For the upright will inhabit the
land,
and those of integrity will
remain in it;
22 but the wicked will be cut off
from the land,

and the treacherous uprooted
from it.

TRUST THE LORD

3 My son, don't forget my
teaching,
but let your heart keep my
commands;
2 for they will bring you
many days, a full life, and well-
being.
3 Never let loyalty and
faithfulness leave you.
Tie them around your neck;
write them on the tablet of
your heart.
4 Then you will find favor and
high regard
in the sight of God and man.

5 Trust in the LORD with all
your heart,
and do not rely on your own
understanding;
6 think about Him in all your
ways,
and He will guide you on the
right paths.
7 Don't consider yourself to be
wise;
fear the LORD and turn away
from evil.
8 This will be healing for your
body
and strengthening for your
bones.
9 Honor the LORD with your
possessions
and with the first produce of
your entire harvest;
10 then your barns will be

completely filled,
and your vats will overflow
with new wine.
11 Do not despise the LORD's
instruction, my son,
and do not loathe His
discipline;
12 for the LORD disciplines the
one He loves,
just as a father, the son he
delights in.

WISDOM BRINGS HAPPINESS

13 Happy is a man who finds
wisdom
and who acquires
understanding,
14 for she is more profitable than
silver,
and her revenue is better than
gold.
15 She is more precious than
jewels;
nothing you desire compares
with her.
16 Long life is in her right hand;
in her left, riches and honor.
17 Her ways are pleasant,
and all her paths, peaceful.
18 She is a tree of life to those who
embrace her,
and those who hold on to her
are happy.

19 The LORD founded the earth
by wisdom
and established the heavens by
understanding.
20 By His knowledge the watery
depths broke open,
and the clouds dripped with dew.

21 Maintain [your] competence
and discretion.
My son, don't lose sight of
them.
22 They will be life for you
and adornment for your neck.
23 Then you will go safely on your
way;
your foot will not stumble.
24 When you lie down, you will
not be afraid;
you will lie down, and your
sleep will be pleasant.
25 Don't fear sudden danger
or the ruin of the wicked when
it comes,
26 for the LORD will be your
confidence
and will keep your foot from a
snare.

TREAT OTHERS FAIRLY

27 When it is in your power,
don't withhold good from the
one to whom it is due.
28 Don't say to your neighbor,
"Go away! Come back later.
I'll give it tomorrow"—when it
is there with you.
29 Don't plan any harm against
your neighbor,
for he trusts you and lives near
you.
30 Don't accuse anyone without
cause,
when he has done you no
harm.
31 Don't envy a violent man
or choose any of his ways;
32 for the devious are detestable
to the LORD,

but He is a friend to the
upright.
33 The LORD's curse is on the
household of the wicked,
but He blesses the home of the
righteous;
34 He mocks those who mock,
but gives grace to the humble.
35 The wise will inherit honor,
but He holds up fools to
dishonor.

A FATHER'S EXAMPLE

4 Listen, [my] sons,
to a father's discipline,
and pay attention so that
you may gain understanding,
2 for I am giving you good
instruction.
Don't abandon my teaching.
3 When I was a son with my
father,
tender and precious to my
mother,
4 he taught me and said:
"Your heart must hold on to
my words.
Keep my commands and live.
5 Get wisdom, get
understanding;
don't forget or turn away from
the words of my mouth.
6 Don't abandon wisdom, and
she will watch over you;
love her, and she will guard you.
7 Wisdom is supreme—so get
wisdom.
And whatever else you get, get
understanding.
8 Cherish her, and she will exalt
you;

if you embrace her, she will
honor you.
9 She will place a garland of
grace on your head;
she will give you a crown of
beauty."

TWO WAYS OF LIFE

10 Listen, my son. Accept my
words,
and you will live many years.
11 I am teaching you the way of
wisdom;
I am guiding you on straight
paths.
12 When you walk, your steps will
not be hindered;
when you run, you will not
stumble.
13 Hold on to instruction; don't
let go.
Guard it, for it is your life.
14 Don't set foot on the path of
the wicked;
don't proceed in the way of evil
ones.
15 Avoid it; don't travel on it.
Turn away from it, and pass it
by.
16 For they can't sleep
unless they have done what is
evil;
they are robbed of sleep unless
they make someone stumble.
17 They eat the bread of
wickedness
and drink the wine of violence.
18 The path of the righteous is like
the light of dawn,
shining brighter and brighter
until midday.

¹⁹ But the way of the wicked is
like the darkest gloom;
they don't know what makes
them stumble.

THE STRAIGHT PATH

²⁰ My son, pay attention to my
words;
listen closely to my sayings.
²¹ Don't lose sight of them;
keep them within your heart.
²² For they are life to those who
find them,
and health to one's whole body.
²³ Guard your heart above all
else,
for it is the source of life.
²⁴ Don't let your mouth speak
dishonestly,
and don't let your lips talk
deviously.
²⁵ Let your eyes look forward;
fix your gaze straight ahead.
²⁶ Carefully consider the path for
your feet,
and all your ways will be
established.
²⁷ Don't turn to the right or to the
left;
keep your feet away from evil.

AVOID SEDUCTION

5 My son, pay attention to my
wisdom;
listen closely to my
understanding
² so that [you] may maintain
discretion
and your lips safeguard
knowledge.
³ Though the lips of the

forbidden woman drip honey
and her words are smoother
than oil,
⁴ in the end she's as bitter as
wormwood
and as sharp as a double-edged
sword.
⁵ Her feet go down to death;
her steps head straight for
Sheol.
⁶ She doesn't consider the path
of life;
she doesn't know that her ways
are unstable.

⁷ So now, [my] sons, listen to me,
and don't turn away from the
words of my mouth.
⁸ Keep your way far from her.
Don't go near the door of her
house.
⁹ Otherwise, you will give up
your vitality to others
and your years to someone
cruel;
¹⁰ strangers will drain your
resources,
and your earnings will end up
in a foreigner's house.
¹¹ At the end of your life, you will
lament
when your physical body has
been consumed,
¹² and you will say, "How I hated
discipline,
and how my heart despised
correction.
¹³ I didn't obey my teachers
or listen closely to my mentors.
¹⁴ I was on the verge of complete
ruin

before the entire community."

ENJOY MARRIAGE

15 Drink water from your own
   cistern,
   water flowing from your own
   well.
16 Should your springs flow in the
   streets,
   streams of water in the public
   squares?
17 They should be for you alone
   and not for you [to share] with
   strangers.
18 Let your fountain be blessed,
   and take pleasure in the wife of
   your youth.
19 A loving doe, a graceful fawn—
   let her breasts always satisfy
   you;
   be lost in her love forever.
20 Why, my son, would you be
   infatuated
   with a forbidden woman
   or embrace the breast of a
   stranger?
21 For a man's ways are before the
   LORD's eyes,
   and He considers all his paths.
22 A wicked man's iniquities
   entrap him;
   he is entangled in the ropes of
   his own sin.
23 He will die because there is no
   instruction,
   and be lost because of his great
   stupidity.

FINANCIAL ENTANGLEMENTS

6 My son, if you have put up
   security for your neighbor
   or entered into an agreement
   with a stranger,
2 you have been trapped by the
   words of your lips—
   ensnared by the words of your
   mouth.
3 Do this, then, my son, and free
   yourself,
   for you have put yourself in
   your neighbor's power:
   Go, humble yourself, and plead
   with your neighbor.
4 Don't give sleep to your eyes
   or slumber to your eyelids.
5 Escape like a gazelle from a
   hunter,
   like a bird from a fowler's trap.

LAZINESS

6 Go to the ant, you slacker!
   Observe its ways and become
   wise.
7 Without leader, administrator,
   or ruler,
8 it prepares its provisions in
   summer;
   it gathers its food during
   harvest.
9 How long will you stay in bed,
   you slacker?
   When will you get up from
   your sleep?
10 A little sleep, a little slumber,
   a little folding of the arms to
   rest,
11 and your poverty will come
   like a robber,
   your need, like a bandit.

THE MALICIOUS MAN

¹² A worthless person, a wicked man,
    who goes around speaking dishonestly,
¹³ who winks his eyes, signals with his feet,
    and gestures with his fingers,
¹⁴ who plots evil with perversity in his heart—
    he stirs up trouble constantly.
¹⁵ Therefore calamity will strike him suddenly;
    he will be shattered instantly—beyond recovery.

WHAT THE *LORD* HATES

¹⁶ Six things the LORD hates;
    in fact, seven are detestable to Him:
¹⁷ arrogant eyes, a lying tongue, hands that shed innocent blood,
¹⁸ a heart that plots wicked schemes,
    feet eager to run to evil,
¹⁹ a lying witness who gives false testimony,
    and one who stirs up trouble among brothers.

WARNING AGAINST ADULTERY

²⁰ My son, keep your father's command,
    and don't reject your mother's teaching.
²¹ Always bind them to your heart;
    tie them around your neck.
²² When you walk here and there, they will guide you;
    when you lie down, they will watch over you;
    when you wake up, they will talk to you.
²³ For a commandment is a lamp, teaching is a light,
    and corrective instructions are the way to life.
²⁴ They will protect you from an evil woman,
    from the flattering tongue of a stranger.
²⁵ Don't lust in your heart for her beauty
    or let her captivate you with her eyelashes.
²⁶ For a prostitute's fee is only a loaf of bread,
    but an adulteress goes after [your] very life.
²⁷ Can a man embrace fire
    and his clothes not be burned?
²⁸ Can a man walk on coals
    without scorching his feet?
²⁹ So it is with the one who sleeps with another man's wife;
    no one who touches her will go unpunished.
³⁰ People don't despise the thief if he steals
    to satisfy himself when he is hungry.
³¹ Still, if caught, he must pay seven times as much;
    he must give up all the wealth in his house.
³² The one who commits adultery lacks sense;
    whoever does so destroys himself.

33 He will get a beating and
    dishonor,
    and his disgrace will never be
    removed.
34 For jealousy enrages a
    husband,
    and he will show no mercy
    when he takes revenge.
35 He will not be appeased by
    anything
    or be persuaded by lavish gifts.

7 My son, obey my words,
    and treasure my commands.
2 Keep my commands and live;
    protect my teachings
    as you would the pupil of your
    eye.
3 Tie them to your fingers;
    write them on the tablet of
    your heart.
4 Say to wisdom, "You are my
    sister,"
    and call understanding [your]
    relative.
5 She will keep you from a
    forbidden woman,
    a stranger with her flattering
    talk.

A STORY OF SEDUCTION

6 At the window of my house
    I looked through my lattice.
7 I saw among the inexperienced,
    I noticed among the youths,
    a young man lacking sense.
8 Crossing the street near her
    corner,
    he strolled down the road to
    her house
9 at twilight, in the evening,

in the dark of the night.
10 A woman came to meet him,
    dressed like a prostitute,
    having a hidden agenda.
11 She is loud and defiant;
    her feet do not stay at home.
12 Now in the street, now in the
    squares,
    she lurks at every corner.
13 She grabs him and kisses him;
    she brazenly says to him,
14 "I've made fellowship offerings;
    today I've fulfilled my vows.
15 So I came out to meet you,
    to search for you, and I've
    found you.
16 I've spread coverings on my
    bed—
    richly colored linen from
    Egypt.
17 I've perfumed my bed
    with myrrh, aloes, and
    cinnamon.
18 Come, let's drink deeply of
    lovemaking until morning.
    Let's feast on each other's love!
19 My husband isn't home;
    he went on a long journey.
20 He took a bag of money with
    him
    and will come home at the time
    of the full moon."
21 She seduces him with her
    persistent pleading;
    she lures with her flattering
    talk.
22 He follows her impulsively
    like an ox going to the
    slaughter,
    like a deer bounding toward a
    trap

²³ until an arrow pierces its liver,
like a bird darting into a snare—
he doesn't know it will cost
him his life.

²⁴ Now, [my] sons, listen to me,
and pay attention to the words
of my mouth.
²⁵ Don't let your heart turn aside
to her ways;
don't stray onto her paths.
²⁶ For she has brought many
down to death;
her victims are countless.
²⁷ Her house is the road to Sheol,
descending to the chambers of
death.

WISDOM'S APPEAL

8 Doesn't Wisdom call out?
Doesn't Understanding make
her voice heard?
² At the heights overlooking the
road,
at the crossroads, she takes her
stand.
³ Beside the gates at the entry to
the city,
at the main entrance, she cries
out:
⁴ "People, I call out to you;
my cry is to mankind.
⁵ Learn to be shrewd, you who
are inexperienced;
develop common sense, you
who are foolish.
⁶ Listen, for I speak of noble
things,
and what my lips say is right.
⁷ For my mouth tells the truth,
and wickedness is detestable

to my lips.
⁸ All the words of my mouth are
righteous;
none of them are deceptive or
perverse.
⁹ All of them are clear to the
perceptive,
and right to those who discover
knowledge.
¹⁰ Accept my instruction instead
of silver,
and knowledge rather than
pure gold.
¹¹ For wisdom is better than
precious stones,
and nothing desirable can
compare with it.
¹² I, Wisdom, share a home with
shrewdness
and have knowledge and
discretion.
¹³ To fear the LORD is to hate
evil.
I hate arrogant pride, evil
conduct,
and perverse speech.
¹⁴ I possess good advice and
competence;
I have understanding and
strength.
¹⁵ It is by me that kings reign
and rulers enact just law;
¹⁶ by me, princes lead,
as do nobles [and] all
righteous judges.
¹⁷ I love those who love me,
and those who search for me
find me.
¹⁸ With me are riches and honor,
lasting wealth and
righteousness.

19 My fruit is better than solid
gold,
and my harvest than pure
silver.
20 I walk in the way of
righteousness,
along the paths of justice,
21 giving wealth as an inheritance
to those who love me,
and filling their treasuries.

22 The LORD made me
at the beginning of His
creation,
before His works of long ago.
23 I was formed before ancient
times,
from the beginning, before the
earth began.
24 I was brought forth
when there were no watery
depths
and no springs filled with
water.
25 I was brought forth
before the mountains and hills
were established,
26 before He made the land, the
fields,
or the first soil on earth.
27 I was there when He
established the heavens,
when He laid out the horizon
on the surface of the ocean,
28 when He placed the skies
above,
when the fountains of the
ocean gushed forth,
29 when He set a limit for the sea
so that the waters would not
violate His command,

when He laid out the
foundations of the earth.
30 I was a skilled craftsman
beside Him.
I was His delight every day,
always rejoicing before Him.
31 I was rejoicing in His inhabited
world,
delighting in the human race.

32 And now, [my] sons, listen to
me;
those who keep my ways are
happy.
33 Listen to instruction and be
wise;
don't ignore it.
34 Anyone who listens to me is
happy,
watching at my doors every
day,
waiting by the posts of my
doorway.
35 For the one who finds me finds
life
and obtains favor from the
LORD,
36 but the one who sins against
me harms himself;
all who hate me love death."

WISDOM VERSUS FOOLISHNESS

9 Wisdom has built her house;
she has carved out her seven
pillars.
2 She has prepared her meat;
she has mixed her wine;
she has also set her table.
3 She has sent out her servants;
she calls out from the highest
points of the city:

4 "Whoever is inexperienced,
enter here!"
To the one who lacks sense, she
says,
5 "Come, eat my bread,
and drink the wine I have
mixed.
6 Leave inexperience behind,
and you will live;
pursue the way of
understanding.
7 The one who corrects a mocker
will bring dishonor on himself;
the one who rebukes a wicked
man will get hurt.
8 Don't rebuke a mocker, or he
will hate you;
rebuke a wise man, and he will
love you.
9 Instruct a wise man, and he
will be wiser still;
teach a righteous man, and he
will learn more.

10 The fear of the LORD is the
beginning of wisdom,
and the knowledge of the Holy
One is understanding.
11 For by Wisdom your days will
be many,
and years will be added to your
life.
12 If you are wise, you are wise for
your own benefit;
if you mock, you alone will
bear [the consequences]."
13 The woman Folly is rowdy;
she is gullible
and knows nothing.
14 She sits by the doorway of her
house,

on a seat at the highest point
of the city,
15 calling to those who pass by,
who go straight ahead
on their paths:
16 "Whoever is inexperienced,
enter here!"
To the one who lacks sense,
she says,
17 "Stolen water is sweet,
and bread [eaten] secretly is
tasty!"
18 But he doesn't know that the
departed spirits are there,
that her guests are in the
depths of Sheol.

A COLLECTION OF SOLOMON'S PROVERBS

10 Solomon's proverbs:

A wise son brings joy to his
father,
but a foolish son, heartache to
his mother.

2 Ill-gotten gains do not profit
anyone,
but righteousness rescues from
death.

3 The LORD will not let the
righteous go hungry,
but He denies the wicked what
they crave.

4 Idle hands make one poor,
but diligent hands bring
riches.

5 The son who gathers during
  summer is prudent;
the son who sleeps during
  harvest is disgraceful.

6 Blessings are on the head of the
  righteous,
but the mouth of the wicked
  conceals violence.

7 The remembrance of the
  righteous is a blessing,
but the name of the wicked will
  rot.

8 A wise heart accepts commands,
  but foolish lips will be
  destroyed.

9 The one who lives with
  integrity lives securely,
but whoever perverts his ways
  will be found out.

10 A sly wink of the eye causes
  grief,
and foolish lips will be
  destroyed.

11 The mouth of the righteous is a
  fountain of life,
but the mouth of the wicked
  conceals violence.

12 Hatred stirs up conflicts,
  but love covers all offenses.

13 Wisdom is found on the lips of
  the discerning,
but a rod is for the back of the
  one who lacks sense.

14 The wise store up knowledge,
  but the mouth of the fool
  hastens destruction.

15 A rich man's wealth is his
  fortified city;
the poverty of the poor is their
  destruction.

16 The labor of the righteous leads
  to life;
the activity of the wicked leads
  to sin.

17 The one who follows
  instruction is on the path to
  life,
but the one who rejects
  correction goes astray.

18 The one who conceals hatred
  has lying lips,
and whoever spreads slander is
  a fool.

19 When there are many words,
  sin is unavoidable,
but the one who controls his
  lips is wise.

20 The tongue of the righteous is
  pure silver;
the heart of the wicked is of
  little value.

21 The lips of the righteous feed
  many,
but fools die for lack of sense.

22 The LORD's blessing enriches,
  and struggle adds nothing to it.

23 As shameful conduct is
pleasure for a fool,
so wisdom is for a man of
understanding.

24 What the wicked dreads will
come to him,
but what the righteous desires
will be given to him.

25 When the whirlwind passes,
the wicked are no more,
but the righteous are secure
forever.

26 Like vinegar to the teeth and
smoke to the eyes,
so the slacker is to the one who
sends him [on an errand].

27 The fear of the LORD prolongs
life,
but the years of the wicked are
cut short.

28 The hope of the righteous is
joy,
but the expectation of the
wicked comes to nothing.

29 The way of the LORD is a
stronghold for the honorable,
but destruction awaits the
malicious.

30 The righteous will never be
shaken,
but the wicked will not remain
on the earth.

31 The mouth of the righteous
produces wisdom,
but a perverse tongue will be
cut out.

32 The lips of the righteous know
what is appropriate,
but the mouth of the wicked,
[only] what is perverse.

11 Dishonest scales are
detestable to the LORD,
but an accurate weight is His
delight.

2 When pride comes, disgrace
follows,
but with humility comes
wisdom.

3 The integrity of the upright
guides them,
but the perversity of the
treacherous destroys them.

4 Wealth is not profitable on a
day of wrath,
but righteousness rescues from
death.

5 The righteousness of the
blameless clears his path,
but the wicked person will fall
because of his wickedness.

6 The righteousness of the
upright rescues them,
but the treacherous are trapped
by their own desires.

7 When the wicked dies,
    his expectation comes to
        nothing,
    and hope placed in wealth
        vanishes.

8 The righteous is rescued from
        trouble;
    in his place, the wicked goes in.

9 With his mouth the ungodly
        destroys his neighbor,
    but through knowledge the
        righteous are rescued.

10 When the righteous thrive, a
        city rejoices,
    and when the wicked die, there
        is joyful shouting.

11 A city is built up by the
        blessing of the upright,
    but it is torn down by the
        mouth of the wicked.

12 Whoever shows contempt for
        his neighbor lacks sense,
    but a man with understanding
        keeps silent.

13 A gossip goes around revealing
        a secret,
    but the trustworthy keeps a
        confidence.

14 Without guidance, people fall,
    but with many counselors
        there is deliverance.

15 If someone puts up security for
        a stranger,

he will suffer for it,
    but the one who hates such
        agreements is protected.

16 A gracious woman gains honor,
    but violent men gain [only]
        riches.

17 A kind man benefits himself,
    but a cruel man brings disaster
        on himself.

18 The wicked man earns an
        empty wage,
    but the one who sows
        righteousness, a true reward.

19 Genuine righteousness [leads]
        to life,
    but pursuing evil [leads] to
        death.

20 Those with twisted minds are
        detestable to the LORD,
    but those with blameless
        conduct are His delight.

21 Be assured that the wicked
        will not go unpunished,
    but the offspring of the
        righteous will escape.

22 A beautiful woman who rejects
        good sense
    is like a gold ring in a pig's
        snout.

23 The desire of the righteous
        [turns out] well,
    but the hope of the wicked
        [leads to] wrath.

²⁴ One person gives freely,
    yet gains more;
    another withholds what is right,
    only to become poor.

²⁵ A generous person will be
    enriched,
    and the one who gives a drink
    of water
    will receive water.

²⁶ People will curse anyone who
    hoards grain,
    but a blessing will come to the
    one who sells it.

²⁷ The one who searches for what
    is good finds favor,
    but if someone looks for
    trouble, it will come to him.

²⁸ Anyone trusting in his riches
    will fall,
    but the righteous will flourish
    like foliage.

²⁹ The one who brings ruin on his
    household
    will inherit the wind,
    and a fool will be a slave
    to someone whose heart is
    wise.

³⁰ The fruit of the righteous is a
    tree of life,
    but violence takes lives.

³¹ If the righteous will be repaid
    on earth,
    how much more the wicked
    and sinful.

12 Whoever loves instruction
    loves knowledge,
    but one who hates correction
    is stupid.

² The good obtain favor from the
    LORD,
    but He condemns a man who
    schemes.

³ Man cannot be made secure by
    wickedness,
    but the root of the righteous is
    immovable.

⁴ A capable wife is her husband's
    crown,
    but a wife who causes shame
    is like rottenness in his bones.

⁵ The thoughts of the righteous
    [are] just,
    but guidance from the wicked
    [leads to] deceit.

⁶ The words of the wicked are a
    deadly ambush,
    but the speech of the upright
    rescues them.

⁷ The wicked are overthrown
    and perish,
    but the house of the righteous
    will stand.

⁸ A man is praised for his
    insight,
    but a twisted mind is despised.

⁹ Better to be dishonored, yet
    have a servant,

than to act important but have
no food.

10 A righteous man cares about
his animal's health,
but [even] the merciful acts of
the wicked are cruel.

11 The one who works his land
will have plenty of food,
but whoever chases fantasies
lacks sense.

12 The wicked desire what evil
men have,
but the root of the righteous
produces [fruit].

13 An evil man is trapped by
[his] rebellious speech,
but the righteous escapes from
trouble.

14 A man will be satisfied with
good
by the words of his mouth,
and the work of a man's hands
will reward him.

15 A fool's way is right in his own
eyes,
but whoever listens to counsel
is wise.

16 A fool's displeasure is known at
once,
but whoever ignores an insult
is sensible.

17 Whoever speaks the truth
declares what is right,

but a false witness, deceit.

18 There is one who speaks rashly,
like a piercing sword;
but the tongue of the wise
[brings] healing.

19 Truthful lips endure forever,
but a lying tongue, only a
moment.

20 Deceit is in the hearts of those
who plot evil,
but those who promote peace
have joy.

21 No disaster [overcomes] the
righteous,
but the wicked are full of
misery.

22 Lying lips are detestable to the
LORD,
but faithful people are His
delight.

23 A shrewd person conceals
knowledge,
but a foolish heart publicizes
stupidity.

24 The diligent hand will rule,
but laziness will lead to forced
labor.

25 Anxiety in a man's heart
weighs it down,
but a good word cheers it up.

26 A righteous man is careful in
dealing with his neighbor,

but the ways of wicked men
   lead them astray.

27 A lazy man doesn't roast his
      game,
   but to a diligent man, his
      wealth is precious.

28 There is life in the path of
      righteousness,
   but another path leads to death.

13 A wise son [hears his]
   father's instruction,
   but a mocker doesn't listen
      to rebuke.

2 From the words of his mouth,
   a man will enjoy good things,
   but treacherous people have an
      appetite for violence.

3 The one who guards his mouth
      protects his life;
   the one who opens his lips
      invites his own ruin.

4 The slacker craves,
      yet has nothing,
   but the diligent is fully
      satisfied.

5 The righteous hate lying,
   but the wicked act disgustingly
      and disgracefully.

6 Righteousness guards people of
      integrity,
   but wickedness undermines
      the sinner.

7 One man pretends to be rich
      but has nothing;
   another pretends to be poor
      but has great wealth.

8 Riches are a ransom for a man's
      life,
   but a poor man hears no threat.

9 The light of the righteous
      shines brightly,
   but the lamp of the wicked is
      extinguished.

10 Arrogance leads to nothing but
      strife,
   but wisdom is gained by those
      who take advice.

11 Wealth obtained by fraud will
      dwindle,
   but whoever earns it through
      labor will multiply it.

12 Delayed hope makes the heart
      sick,
   but fulfilled desire is a tree of
      life.

13 The one who has contempt
      for instruction will pay the
      penalty,
   but the one who respects a
      command will be rewarded.

14 A wise man's instruction is a
      fountain of life,
   turning people away from the
      snares of death.

¹⁵ Good sense wins favor,
but the way of the treacherous
never changes.

¹⁶ Every sensible person acts
knowledgeably,
but a fool displays his stupidity.

¹⁷ A wicked messenger falls into
trouble,
but a trustworthy courier
[brings] healing.

¹⁸ Poverty and disgrace [come to]
those
who ignore instruction,
but the one who accepts rebuke
will be honored.

¹⁹ Desire fulfilled is sweet to the
taste,
but fools hate to turn from evil.

²⁰ The one who walks with the
wise will become wise,
but a companion of fools will
suffer harm.

²¹ Disaster pursues sinners,
but good rewards the
righteous.

²² A good man leaves
an inheritance to his
grandchildren,
but the sinner's wealth is stored
up for the righteous.

²³ The field of the poor yields
abundant food,
but without justice,

it is swept away.

²⁴ The one who will not use the
rod hates his son,
but the one who loves him
disciplines him diligently.

²⁵ A righteous man eats
until he is satisfied,
but the stomach of the wicked
is empty.

14 Every wise woman builds
her house,
but a foolish one tears it down
with her own hands.

² Whoever lives with integrity
fears the LORD,
but the one who is devious in
his ways despises Him.

³ The proud speech of a fool
[brings] a rod [of discipline],
but the lips of the wise protect
them.

⁴ Where there are no oxen, the
feeding-trough is empty,
but an abundant harvest [comes]
through the strength of an ox.

⁵ An honest witness does not
deceive,
but a dishonest witness utters
lies.

⁶ A mocker seeks wisdom and
doesn't find it,
but knowledge [comes] easily
to the perceptive.

⁷ Stay away from a foolish man;
  you will gain no knowledge
  from his speech.

⁸ The sensible man's wisdom is
  to consider his way,
  but the stupidity of fools
  deceives [them].

⁹ Fools mock at making
  restitution,
  but there is goodwill among
  the upright.

¹⁰ The heart knows its own
  bitterness,
  and no outsider shares in its
  joy.

¹¹ The house of the wicked will be
  destroyed,
  but the tent of the upright
  will stand.

¹² There is a way that seems right
  to a man,
  but its end is the way to death.

¹³ Even in laughter a heart may be
  sad,
  and joy may end in grief.

¹⁴ The disloyal will get what their
  conduct deserves,
  and a good man,
  what his [deeds deserve].

¹⁵ The inexperienced believe
  anything,
  but the sensible watch their
  steps.

¹⁶ A wise man is cautious and
  turns from evil,
  but a fool is easily angered and
  is careless.

¹⁷ A quick-tempered man acts
  foolishly,
  and a man who schemes is
  hated.

¹⁸ The gullible inherit foolishness,
  but the sensible are crowned
  with knowledge.

¹⁹ The evil bow before those who
  are good,
  the wicked, at the gates of the
  righteous.

²⁰ A poor man is hated even by
  his neighbor,
  but there are many who love
  the rich.

²¹ The one who despises his
  neighbor sins,
  but whoever shows kindness to
  the poor will be happy.

²² Don't those who plan evil go
  astray?
  But those who plan good find
  loyalty and faithfulness.

²³ There is profit in all hard work,
  but endless talk leads only to
  poverty.

²⁴ The crown of the wise is their
  wealth,
  but the foolishness of fools

produces foolishness.

25 A truthful witness rescues
    lives,
  but one who utters lies is
    deceitful.

26 In the fear of the LORD one has
    strong confidence
  and his children have a refuge.

27 The fear of the LORD is a
    fountain of life,
  turning people from the snares
    of death.

28 A large population is a king's
    splendor,
  but a shortage of people is a
    ruler's devastation.

29 A patient person [shows] great
    understanding,
  but a quick-tempered one
    promotes foolishness.

30 A tranquil heart is life to the
    body,
  but jealousy is rottenness to the
    bones.

31 The one who oppresses the
    poor insults their Maker,
  but one who is kind to the
    needy honors Him.

32 The wicked are thrown down
    by their own sin,
  but the righteous have a refuge
    when they die.

33 Wisdom resides in the heart of
    the discerning;
  she is known even among fools.

34 Righteousness exalts a nation,
  but sin is a disgrace to any
    people.

35 A king favors a wise servant,
  but his anger falls on a
    disgraceful one.

15 A gentle answer turns away
    anger,
  but a harsh word stirs up
    wrath.

2 The tongue of the wise makes
    knowledge attractive,
  but the mouth of fools blurts
    out foolishness.

3 The eyes of the LORD are
    everywhere,
  observing the wicked and the
    good.

4 The tongue that heals is a tree
    of life,
  but a devious tongue breaks
    the spirit.

5 A fool despises his father's
    instruction,
  but a person who heeds
    correction is sensible.

6 The house of the righteous has
    great wealth,
  but trouble accompanies the
    income of the wicked.

⁷ The lips of the wise broadcast
knowledge,
but not so the heart of fools.

⁸ The sacrifice of the wicked is
detestable to the LORD,
but the prayer of the upright is
His delight.

⁹ The LORD detests the way of
the wicked,
but He loves the one who
pursues righteousness.

¹⁰ Discipline is harsh for the one
who leaves the path;
the one who hates correction
will die.

¹¹ Sheol and Abaddon lie open
before the LORD—
how much more, human hearts.

¹² A mocker doesn't love one who
corrects him;
he will not consult the wise.

¹³ A joyful heart makes a face
cheerful,
but a sad heart [produces] a
broken spirit.

¹⁴ A discerning mind seeks
knowledge,
but the mouth of fools feeds on
foolishness.

¹⁵ All the days of the oppressed
are miserable,
but a cheerful heart has a
continual feast.

¹⁶ Better a little with the fear of
the LORD
than great treasure with
turmoil.

¹⁷ Better a meal of vegetables
where there is love
than a fattened calf with
hatred.

¹⁸ A hot-tempered man stirs up
conflict,
but a man slow to anger calms
strife.

¹⁹ A slacker's way is like a thorny
hedge,
but the path of the upright is a
highway.

²⁰ A wise son brings joy to his
father,
but a foolish one despises his
mother.

²¹ Foolishness brings joy to one
without sense,
but a man with understanding
walks a straight path.

²² Plans fail when there is no
counsel,
but with many advisers they
succeed.

²³ A man takes joy in giving an
answer;
and a timely word—how good
that is!

24 For the discerning the path of
   life leads upward,
   so that he may avoid going
   down to Sheol.

25 The LORD destroys the house
   of the proud,
   but He protects the widow's
   territory.

26 The LORD detests the plans of
   an evil man,
   but pleasant words are pure.

27 The one who profits
   dishonestly troubles his
   household,
   but the one who hates bribes
   will live.

28 The mind of the righteous
   person thinks before
   answering,
   but the mouth of the wicked
   blurts out evil things.

29 The LORD is far from the
   wicked,
   but He hears the prayer of the
   righteous.

30 Bright eyes cheer the heart;
   good news strengthens the
   bones.

31 An ear that listens to life-
   giving rebukes
   will be at home among the
   wise.

32 Anyone who ignores
   instruction despises himself,
   but whoever listens to
   correction acquires good
   sense.

33 The fear of the LORD is
   wisdom's instruction,
   and humility comes before
   honor.

16 The reflections of the heart
   belong to man,
   but the answer of the tongue is
   from the LORD.

2 All a man's ways seem right in
   his own eyes,
   but the LORD weighs the
   motives.

3 Commit your activities to the
   LORD
   and your plans will be
   achieved.

4 The LORD has prepared
   everything for His purpose—
   even the wicked for the day of
   disaster.

5 Everyone with a proud heart is
   detestable to the LORD;
   be assured, he will not go
   unpunished.

6 Wickedness is atoned for by
   loyalty and faithfulness,
   and one turns from evil by the
   fear of the LORD.

7 When a man's ways please the
   LORD,
   He makes even his enemies to
   be at peace with him.

8 Better a little with
   righteousness
   than great income with injustice.

9 A man's heart plans his way,
   but the LORD determines his
   steps.

10 God's verdict is on the lips of a
    king;
    his mouth should not err in
    judgment.

11 Honest balances and scales are
    the LORD's;
    all the weights in the bag are
    His concern.

12 Wicked behavior is detestable
    to kings,
    since a throne is established
    through righteousness.

13 Righteous lips are a king's
    delight,
    and he loves one who speaks
    honestly.

14 A king's fury is a messenger of
    death,
    but a wise man appeases it.

15 When a king's face lights up,
    there is life;
    his favor is like a cloud with
    spring rain.

16 Acquire wisdom—
    how much better it is than
    gold!
    And acquire understanding—
    it is preferable to silver.

17 The highway of the upright
    avoids evil;
    the one who guards his way
    protects his life.

18 Pride comes before
    destruction,
    and an arrogant spirit before a
    fall.

19 Better to be lowly of spirit with
    the humble
    than to divide plunder with the
    proud.

20 The one who understands a
    matter finds success,
    and the one who trusts in the
    LORD will be happy.

21 Anyone with a wise heart is
    called discerning,
    and pleasant speech increases
    learning.

22 Insight is a fountain of life for
    its possessor,
    but folly is the instruction of
    fools.

23 A wise heart instructs its
    mouth
    and increases learning with its
    speech.

²⁴ Pleasant words are a
   honeycomb:
   sweet to the taste and health to
   the body.

²⁵ There is a way that seems right
   to a man,
   but in the end it is the way of
   death.

²⁶ A worker's appetite works for
   him
   because his hunger urges
   him on.

²⁷ A worthless man digs up evil,
   and his speech is like a
   scorching fire.

²⁸ A contrary man spreads
   conflict,
   and a gossip separates friends.

²⁹ A violent man lures his
   neighbor,
   leading him in a way that is not
   good.

³⁰ The one who narrows his eyes
   is planning deceptions;
   the one who compresses his
   lips brings about evil.

³¹ Gray hair is a glorious crown;
   it is found in the way of
   righteousness.

³² Patience is better than power,
   and controlling one's temper,
   than capturing a city.

³³ The lot is cast into the lap,
   but its every decision is from
   the LORD.

17 Better a dry crust with peace
   than a house full of feasting
   with strife.

² A wise servant will rule over a
   disgraceful son
   and share an inheritance
   among brothers.

³ A crucible is for silver and a
   smelter for gold,
   but the LORD is a tester of
   hearts.

⁴ A wicked person listens to
   malicious talk;
   a liar pays attention to a
   destructive tongue.

⁵ The one who mocks the poor
   insults his Maker,
   and one who rejoices over
   disaster
   will not go unpunished.

⁶ Grandchildren are the crown
   of the elderly,
   and the pride of sons is their
   fathers.

⁷ Excessive speech is not
   appropriate on a fool's lips;
   how much worse are lies for a
   ruler.

⁸ A bribe seems like a magic
   stone to its owner;

wherever he turns, he succeeds.

9 Whoever conceals an offense
  promotes love,
  but whoever gossips about it
  separates friends.

10 A rebuke cuts into a perceptive
   person
   more than a hundred lashes
   into a fool.

11 An evil man seeks only
   rebellion;
   a cruel messenger will be sent
   against him.

12 Better for a man to meet a bear
   robbed of her cubs
   than a fool in his foolishness.

13 If anyone returns evil for good,
   evil will never depart from his
   house.

14 To start a conflict is to release a
   flood;
   stop the dispute before it
   breaks out.

15 Acquitting the guilty and
   condemning the just—
   both are detestable to the
   LORD.

16 Why does a fool have money in
   his hand
   with no intention of buying
   wisdom?

17 A friend loves at all times,
   and a brother is born for a
   difficult time.

18 One without sense enters an
   agreement
   and puts up security for his
   friend.

19 One who loves to offend loves
   strife;
   one who builds a high
   threshold invites injury.

20 One with a twisted mind will
   not succeed,
   and one with deceitful speech
   will fall into ruin.

21 A man fathers a fool to his own
   sorrow;
   the father of a fool has no joy.

22 A joyful heart is good
   medicine,
   but a broken spirit dries up the
   bones.

23 A wicked man secretly takes a
   bribe
   to subvert the course of justice.

24 Wisdom is the focus of the
   perceptive,
   but a fool's eyes roam to the
   ends of the earth.

25 A foolish son is grief to his
   father
   and bitterness to the one who
   bore him.

26 It is certainly not good to fine
an innocent person,
or to beat a noble for his
honesty.

27 The intelligent person restrains
his words,
and one who keeps a cool head
is a man of understanding.

28 Even a fool is considered wise
when he keeps silent,
discerning, when he seals his
lips.

18 One who isolates himself
pursues [selfish] desires;
he rebels against all sound
judgment.

2 A fool does not delight in
understanding,
but only wants to show off his
opinions.

3 When a wicked man comes,
shame does also,
and along with dishonor,
disgrace.

4 The words of a man's mouth
are deep waters,
a flowing river, a fountain of
wisdom.

5 It is not good to show partiality
to the guilty
by perverting the justice due
the innocent.

6 A fool's lips lead to strife,
and his mouth provokes a
beating.

7 A fool's mouth is his devastation,
and his lips are a trap for his
life.

8 A gossip's words are like choice
food
that goes down to one's
innermost being.

9 The one who is truly lazy in his
work
is brother to a vandal.

10 The name of the LORD is a
strong tower;
the righteous run to it and are
protected.

11 A rich man's wealth is his
fortified city;
in his imagination it is like a
high wall.

12 Before his downfall a man's
heart is proud,
but before honor comes
humility.

13 The one who gives an answer
before he listens—
this is foolishness and disgrace
for him.

14 A man's spirit can endure
sickness,
but who can survive a broken
spirit?

¹⁵ The mind of the discerning
acquires knowledge,
and the ear of the wise seeks it.

¹⁶ A gift opens doors for a man
and brings him before the
great.

¹⁷ The first to state his case seems
right
until another comes and
cross-examines him.

¹⁸ [Casting] the lot ends quarrels
and separates powerful
opponents.

¹⁹ An offended brother is [harder
to reach]
than a fortified city,
and quarrels are like the bars
of a fortress.

²⁰ From the fruit of his mouth a
man's stomach is satisfied;
he is filled with the product of
his lips.

²¹ Life and death are in the power
of the tongue,
and those who love it will eat
its fruit.

²² A man who finds a wife finds a
good thing
and obtains favor from the
LORD.

²³ The poor man pleads,
but the rich one answers
roughly.

²⁴ A man with many friends may
be harmed,
but there is a friend who stays
closer than a brother.

19 Better a poor man who walks
in integrity
than someone who has
deceitful lips and is a fool.

² Even zeal is not good without
knowledge,
and the one who acts hastily
sins.

³ A man's own foolishness leads
him astray,
yet his heart rages against the
LORD.

⁴ Wealth attracts many friends,
but a poor man is separated
from his friend.

⁵ A false witness will not go
unpunished,
and one who utters lies will not
escape.

⁶ Many seek the favor of a ruler,
and everyone is a friend of one
who gives gifts.

⁷ All the brothers of a poor man
hate him;
how much more do his friends
keep their distance from him!
He may pursue [them with]
words,
[but] they are not [there].

8 The one who acquires good
   sense loves himself;
one who safeguards
   understanding finds success.

9 A false witness will not go
   unpunished,
and one who utters lies
   perishes.

10 Luxury is not appropriate for a
    fool—
how much less for a slave to
    rule over princes!

11 A person's insight gives him
    patience,
and his virtue is to overlook an
    offense.

12 A king's rage is like a lion's
    roar,
but his favor is like dew on the
    grass.

13 A foolish son is his father's
    ruin,
and a wife's nagging is an
    endless dripping.

14 A house and wealth are
    inherited from fathers,
but a sensible wife is from the
    LORD.

15 Laziness induces deep sleep,
and a lazy person will go
    hungry.

16 The one who keeps commands
    preserves himself;

one who disregards his ways
   will die.

17 Kindness to the poor is a loan
    to the LORD,
and He will give a reward to
    the lender.

18 Discipline your son while there
    is hope;
don't be intent on killing him.

19 A person with great anger
    bears the penalty;
if you rescue him, you'll have
    to do it again.

20 Listen to counsel and receive
    instruction
so that you may be wise in later
    life.

21 Many plans are in a man's
    heart,
but the LORD's decree will
    prevail.

22 A man's desire should be
    loyalty to the covenant;
better to be a poor man than a
    perjurer.

23 The fear of the LORD leads to
    life;
one will sleep at night without
    danger.

24 The slacker buries his hand in
    the bowl;
he doesn't even bring it back to
    his mouth.

²⁵ Strike a mocker, and the
inexperienced learn a lesson;
rebuke the discerning, and he
gains knowledge.

²⁶ The one who assaults his father
and evicts his mother
is a disgraceful and shameful
son.

²⁷ If you stop listening to
instruction, my son,
you will stray from the words
of knowledge.

²⁸ A worthless witness mocks
justice,
and a wicked mouth swallows
iniquity.

²⁹ Judgments are prepared for
mockers,
and beatings for the backs of
fools.

20 Wine is a mocker, beer is a
brawler,
and whoever staggers because
of them is not wise.

² A king's terrible wrath is like
the roaring of a lion;
anyone who provokes him
endangers himself.

³ It is honorable for a man to
resolve a dispute,
but any fool can get himself
into a quarrel.

⁴ The slacker does not plow
during planting season;
at harvest time he looks, and
there is nothing.

⁵ Counsel in a man's heart is
deep water;
but a man of understanding
draws it up.

⁶ Many a man proclaims his own
loyalty,
but who can find a trustworthy
man?

⁷ The one who lives with
integrity is righteous;
his children who come after
him will be happy.

⁸ A king sitting on a throne
to judge
sifts out all evil with his eyes.

⁹ Who can say, "I have kept my
heart pure;
I am cleansed from my sin"?

¹⁰ Differing weights and varying
measures—
both are detestable to the
LORD.

¹¹ Even a young man is known by
his actions—
by whether his behavior is pure
and upright.

¹² The hearing ear
and the seeing eye—
the LORD made them both.

¹³ Don't love sleep, or you will
become poor;
open your eyes, and you'll have
enough to eat.

¹⁴ "It's worthless, it's worthless!"
the buyer says,
but after he is on his way, he
gloats.

¹⁵ There is gold and a multitude
of jewels,
but knowledgeable lips are a
rare treasure.

¹⁶ Take his garment,
for he has put up security for
a stranger;
get collateral if it is for
foreigners.

¹⁷ Food gained by fraud is sweet
to a man,
but afterwards his mouth is full
of gravel.

¹⁸ Finalize plans through counsel,
and wage war with sound
guidance.

¹⁹ The one who reveals secrets is a
constant gossip;
avoid someone with a big
mouth.

²⁰ Whoever curses his father or
mother—
his lamp will go out in deep
darkness.

²¹ An inheritance gained
prematurely
will not be blessed ultimately.

²² Don't say, "I will avenge this
evil!"
Wait on the LORD, and He will
rescue you.

²³ Differing weights are detestable
to the LORD,
and dishonest scales are unfair.

²⁴ A man's steps are determined
by the LORD,
so how can anyone understand
his own way?

²⁵ It is a trap for anyone to
dedicate something rashly
and later to reconsider his
vows.

²⁶ A wise king separates out the
wicked
and drives the threshing wheel
over them.

²⁷ A person's breath is the lamp of
the LORD,
searching the innermost parts.

²⁸ Loyalty and faithfulness
deliver a king;
through loyalty he maintains
his throne.

²⁹ The glory of young men is their
strength,
and the splendor of old men is
gray hair.

³⁰ Lashes and wounds purge away
   evil,
   and beatings cleanse the
   innermost parts.

21 A king's heart is a water
   channel in the LORD's hand:
   He directs it wherever He
   chooses.

² All the ways of a man seem
   right to him,
   but the LORD evaluates the
   motives.

³ Doing what is righteous and
   just
   is more acceptable to the LORD
   than sacrifice.

⁴ The lamp that guides the
   wicked—
   haughty eyes and an arrogant
   heart—is sin.

⁵ The plans of the diligent
   certainly lead to profit,
   but anyone who is reckless only
   becomes poor.

⁶ Making a fortune through a
   lying tongue
   is a vanishing mist, a pursuit of
   death.

⁷ The violence of the wicked
   sweeps them away
   because they refuse to act
   justly.

⁸ A guilty man's conduct is
   crooked,
   but the behavior of the
   innocent is upright.

⁹ Better to live on the corner of a
   roof
   than to share a house with a
   nagging wife.

¹⁰ A wicked person desires evil;
   he has no consideration for his
   neighbor.

¹¹ When a mocker is punished,
   the inexperienced become
   wiser;
   when one teaches a wise man,
   he acquires knowledge.

¹² The Righteous One considers
   the house of the wicked;
   He brings the wicked to ruin.

¹³ The one who shuts his ears to
   the cry of the poor
   will himself also call out and
   not be answered.

¹⁴ A secret gift soothes anger,
   and a covert bribe, fierce rage.

¹⁵ Justice executed is a joy to the
   righteous
   but a terror to those who
   practice iniquity.

¹⁶ The man who strays from the
   way of wisdom
   will come to rest
   in the assembly

of the departed spirits.

17 The one who loves pleasure will
   become a poor man;
   whoever loves wine and oil will
   not get rich.

18 The wicked are a ransom for
   the righteous,
   and the treacherous, for the
   upright.

19 Better to live in a wilderness
   than with a nagging and hot-
   tempered wife.

20 Precious treasure and oil are in
   the dwelling of the wise,
   but a foolish man consumes
   them.

21 The one who pursues
   righteousness and faithful
   love
   will find life, righteousness,
   and honor.

22 The wise conquer a city of
   warriors
   and bring down its mighty
   fortress.

23 The one who guards his mouth
   and tongue
   keeps himself out of trouble.

24 The proud and arrogant
   person, named "Mocker,"
   acts with excessive pride.

25 A slacker's craving will kill him
   because his hands refuse to
   work.

26 He is filled with craving all day
   long,
   but the righteous give and
   don't hold back.

27 The sacrifice of a wicked
   person is detestable—
   how much more so
   when he brings it with ulterior
   motives!

28 A lying witness will perish,
   but the one who listens will
   speak successfully.

29 A wicked man puts on a bold
   face,
   but the upright man considers
   his way.

30 No wisdom, no understanding,
   and no counsel
   [will prevail] against the
   LORD.

31 A horse is prepared for the day
   of battle,
   but victory comes from the
   LORD.

22 A good name is to be chosen
   over great wealth;
   favor is better than silver and
   gold.

2 The rich and the poor have this
   in common:
   the LORD made them both.

³ A sensible person sees danger
   and takes cover,
   but the inexperienced keep
   going and are punished.

⁴ The result of humility is fear of
   the LORD,
   along with wealth, honor, and
   life.

⁵ There are thorns and snares on
   the path of the crooked;
   the one who guards himself
   stays far from them.

⁶ Teach a youth about the way he
   should go;
   even when he is old he will not
   depart from it.

⁷ The rich rule over the poor,
   and the borrower is a slave to
   the lender.

⁸ The one who sows injustice will
   reap disaster,
   and the rod of his fury will be
   destroyed.

⁹ A generous person will be
   blessed,
   for he shares his food with the
   poor.

¹⁰ Drive out a mocker, and
   conflict goes too;
   then lawsuits and dishonor will
   cease.

¹¹ The one who loves a pure heart
   and gracious lips—the king is
   his friend.

¹² The LORD's eyes keep watch
   over knowledge,
   but He overthrows the words
   of the treacherous.

¹³ The slacker says,
   "There's a lion outside!
   I'll be killed in the streets!"

¹⁴ The mouth of the forbidden
   woman is a deep pit;
   a man cursed by the LORD will
   fall into it.

¹⁵ Foolishness is tangled up in the
   heart of a youth;
   the rod of discipline will drive
   it away from him.

¹⁶ Oppressing the poor to enrich
   oneself,
   and giving to the rich—both
   lead only to poverty.

WORDS OF THE WISE

¹⁷ Listen closely, pay attention to
   the words of the wise,
   and apply your mind to my
   knowledge.

¹⁸ For it is pleasing if you keep
   them within you
   and if they are constantly on
   your lips.

¹⁹ I have instructed you today—
   even you—
   so that your confidence may be
   in the LORD.

²⁰ Haven't I written for you
   thirty sayings
   about counsel and knowledge,

²¹ in order to teach you true and

reliable words,
so that you may give a
dependable report
to those who sent you?

22 Don't rob a poor man because
he is poor,
and don't crush the oppressed
at the gate,
23 for the LORD will take up their
case
and will plunder those who
plunder them.

24 Don't make friends with an
angry man,
and don't be a companion
of a hot-tempered man,
25 or you will learn his ways
and entangle yourself in a
snare.

26 Don't be one of those who
enter agreements,
who put up security for loans.
27 If you have no money to pay,
even your bed will be taken
from under you.

28 Don't move an ancient
property line
that your fathers set up.

29 Do you see a man skilled in his
work?
He will stand in the presence of
kings.
He will not stand in the
presence of unknown men.

23 When you sit down to dine
with a ruler,
consider carefully what is
before you,
2 and stick a knife in your throat
if you have a big appetite;
3 don't desire his choice food,
for that food is deceptive.

4 Don't wear yourself out to get
rich;
stop giving your attention to it.
5 As soon as your eyes fly to it, it
disappears,
for it makes wings for itself
and flies like an eagle to the sky.

6 Don't eat a stingy person's
bread,
and don't desire his choice
food,
7 for as he thinks within himself,
so he is.
"Eat and drink," he says to you,
but his heart is not with you.
8 You will vomit the little you've
eaten
and waste your pleasant words.

9 Don't speak to a fool,
for he will despise the insight
of your words.

10 Don't move an ancient
property line,
and don't encroach on the
fields of the fatherless,

11 for their Redeemer is strong,
and He will take up their case
against you.

¹² Apply yourself to instruction
and listen to words of
knowledge.

¹³ Don't withhold correction
from a youth;
if you beat him with a rod, he
will not die.
¹⁴ Strike him with a rod,
and you will rescue his life
from Sheol.

¹⁵ My son, if your heart is wise,
my heart will indeed rejoice.
¹⁶ My innermost being will cheer
when your lips say what is
right.

¹⁷ Don't be jealous of sinners;
instead, always fear the LORD.
¹⁸ For then you will have a future,
and your hope will never fade.

¹⁹ Listen, my son, and be wise;
keep your mind on the right
course.
²⁰ Don't associate with those who
drink too much wine,
or with those who gorge
themselves on meat.
²¹ For the drunkard and the
glutton will become poor,
and grogginess will clothe
[them] in rags.

²² Listen to your father who gave
you life,
and don't despise your mother
when she is old.
²³ Buy—and do not sell—truth,
wisdom, instruction, and
understanding.
²⁴ The father of a righteous son
will rejoice greatly,
and one who fathers a wise son
will delight in him.
²⁵ Let your father and mother
have joy,
and let her who gave birth to
you rejoice.

²⁶ My son, give me your heart,
and let your eyes observe my
ways.
²⁷ For a prostitute is a deep pit,
and a forbidden woman is a
narrow well;
²⁸ indeed, she sets an ambush like
a robber
and increases those among
men who are unfaithful.

²⁹ Who has woe?
Who has sorrow?
Who has conflicts?
Who has complaints?
Who has wounds for no
reason?
Who has red eyes?
³⁰ Those who linger over wine,
those who go looking for
mixed wine.
³¹ Don't gaze at wine when it is
red,
when it gleams in the cup
and goes down smoothly.
³² In the end it bites like a snake
and stings like a viper.
³³ Your eyes will see strange
things,
and you will say absurd things.
³⁴ You'll be like someone sleeping

out at sea
or lying down on the top of a
ship's mast.

35 "They struck me, but I feel no
pain!
They beat me, but I didn't
know it!
When will I wake up?
I'll look for another [drink]."

24 Don't envy evil men
or desire to be with them,
2 for their hearts plan violence,
and their words stir up trouble.

3 A house is built by wisdom,
and it is established by
understanding;
4 by knowledge the rooms are
filled
with every precious and
beautiful treasure.

5 A wise warrior is better than a
strong one,
and a man of knowledge than
one of strength;
6 for you should wage war with
sound guidance—
victory comes with many
counselors.

7 Wisdom is inaccessible to a
fool;
he does not open his mouth at
the gate.
8 The one who plots evil
will be called a schemer.
9 A foolish scheme is sin,
and a mocker is detestable to
people.

10 If you do nothing in a difficult
time,
your strength is limited.
11 Rescue those being taken off to
death,
and save those stumbling
toward slaughter.
12 If you say, "But we didn't know
about this,"
won't He who weighs hearts
consider it?
Won't He who protects your
life know?
Won't He repay a person
according to his work?

13 Eat honey, my son, for it is
good,
and the honeycomb is sweet to
your palate;
14 realize that wisdom is the same
for you.
If you find it, you will have a
future,
and your hope will never fade.

15 Don't set an ambush, wicked
man,
at the camp of the righteous
man;
don't destroy his dwelling.
16 Though a righteous man falls
seven times,
he will get up,
but the wicked will stumble
into ruin.

17 Don't gloat when your enemy
falls,
and don't let your heart rejoice
when he stumbles,

18 or the LORD will see, be
    displeased,
  and turn His wrath away from
    him.

19 Don't worry because of
    evildoers,
  and don't envy the wicked.
20 For the evil have no future;
  the lamp of the wicked will be
    put out.

21 My son, fear the LORD, as well
    as the king,
  and don't associate with rebels,
22 for their destruction will come
    suddenly;
  who knows what disaster these
    two can bring?

23 These [sayings] also belong to
    the wise:

  It is not good to show partiality
    in judgment.
24 Whoever says to the guilty,
    "You are innocent"—
  people will curse him, and
    tribes will denounce him;
25 but it will go well with those
    who convict the guilty,
  and a generous blessing will
    come to them.

26 He who gives an honest answer
  gives a kiss on the lips.

27 Complete your outdoor work,
    and prepare your field;
  afterwards, build your house.

28 Don't testify against your
    neighbor without cause.
  Don't deceive with your lips.
29 Don't say, "I'll do to him what
    he did to me;
  I'll repay the man for what he
    has done."

30 I went by the field of a slacker
  and by the vineyard of a man
    lacking sense.
31 Thistles had come up
    everywhere,
  weeds covered the ground,
  and the stone wall was ruined.
32 I saw, and took it to heart;
  I looked, and received
    instruction:
33 a little sleep, a little slumber,
  a little folding of the arms to
    rest,
34 and your poverty will come
    like a robber,
  your need, like a bandit.

HEZEKIAH'S COLLECTION

25 These too are proverbs of
    Solomon,
  which the men of Hezekiah,
    king of Judah, copied.

2 It is the glory of God to conceal
    a matter
  and the glory of kings to
    investigate a matter.
3 As the heaven is high and the
    earth is deep,
  so the hearts of kings cannot
    be investigated.

4 Remove impurities from silver,

199

and a vessel will be produced
for a silversmith.
5 Remove the wicked from the
king's presence,
and his throne will be
established in righteousness.

6 Don't brag about yourself
before the king,
and don't stand in the place of
the great;
7 for it is better for him to say to
you, "Come up here!"
than to demote you in plain
view of a noble.

8 Don't take a matter to court
hastily.
Otherwise, what will you do
afterwards
if your opponent humiliates
you?
9 Make your case with your
opponent
without revealing another's
secret;
10 otherwise, the one who hears
will disgrace you,
and you'll never live it down.

11 A word spoken at the right time
is like golden apples on a silver
tray.
12 A wise correction to a receptive
ear
is like a gold ring or an
ornament of gold.

13 To those who send him, a
trustworthy messenger
is like the coolness of snow on
a harvest day;
he refreshes the life of his
masters.

14 The man who boasts about a
gift that does not exist
is like clouds and wind without
rain.
15 A ruler can be persuaded
through patience,
and a gentle tongue can break a
bone.
16 If you find honey, eat only what
you need;
otherwise, you'll get sick from
it and vomit.
17 Seldom set foot in your
neighbor's house;
otherwise, he'll get sick of you
and hate you.

18 A man giving false testimony
against his neighbor
is like a club, a sword, or a
sharp arrow.
19 Trusting an unreliable person
in a time of trouble
is like a rotten tooth or a
faltering foot.

20 Singing songs to a troubled
heart
is like taking off clothing on a
cold day,
or like [pouring] vinegar on
soda.

21 If your enemy is hungry, give
him food to eat,
and if he is thirsty, give him
water to drink;

22 for you will heap coals on his head,
and the LORD will reward you.

23 The north wind produces rain,
and a backbiting tongue, angry looks.
24 Better to live on the corner of a roof
than in a house shared with a nagging wife.
25 Good news from a distant land
is like cold water to a parched throat.
26 A righteous person who yields to the wicked
is like a muddied spring or a polluted well.
27 It is not good to eat too much honey,
or to seek glory after glory.
28 A man who does not control his temper
is like a city whose wall is broken down.

26 Like snow in summer and rain at harvest,
honor is inappropriate for a fool.
2 Like a flitting sparrow or a fluttering swallow,
an undeserved curse goes nowhere.
3 A whip for the horse, a bridle for the donkey,
and a rod for the backs of fools.
4 Don't answer a fool according to his foolishness,
or you'll be like him yourself.
5 Answer a fool according to his foolishness,
or he'll become wise in his own eyes.
6 The one who sends a message by a fool's hand
cuts off his own feet and drinks violence.
7 A proverb in the mouth of a fool
is like lame legs that hang limp.
8 Giving honor to a fool
is like binding a stone in a sling.
9 A proverb in the mouth of a fool
is like a stick with thorns,
brandished by the hand of a drunkard.
10 The one who hires a fool, or who hires those passing by,
is like an archer who wounds everyone.
11 As a dog returns to its vomit,
so a fool repeats his foolishness.
12 Do you see a man who is wise in his own eyes?
There is more hope for a fool than for him.

13 The slacker says, "There's a lion in the road—
a lion in the public square!"
14 A door turns on its hinge,
and a slacker, on his bed.
15 The slacker buries his hand in the bowl;
he is too weary to bring it to his mouth.
16 In his own eyes, a slacker is wiser

than seven men who can
answer sensibly.

17 A passerby who meddles in a
quarrel that's not his
is like one who grabs a dog by
the ears.

18 Like a madman who throws
flaming darts and deadly
arrows,

19 so is the man who deceives his
neighbor
and says, "I was only joking!"

20 Without wood, fire goes out;
without a gossip, conflict dies
down.

21 As charcoal for embers and
wood for fire,
so is a quarrelsome man for
kindling strife.

22 A gossip's words are like choice
food
that goes down to one's
innermost being.

23 Smooth lips with an evil heart
are like glaze on an earthen
vessel.

24 A hateful person disguises
himself with his speech
and harbors deceit within.

25 When he speaks graciously,
don't believe him,
for there are seven
abominations in his heart.

26 Though his hatred is concealed
by deception,
his evil will be revealed in the
assembly.

27 The one who digs a pit will fall

into it,
and whoever rolls a stone—
it will come back on him.

28 A lying tongue hates those it
crushes,
and a flattering mouth causes
ruin.

27 Don't boast about tomorrow,
for you don't know what a day
might bring.

2 Let another praise you, and not
your own mouth—
a stranger, and not your own lips.

3 A stone is heavy and sand,
a burden,
but aggravation from a fool
outweighs them both.

4 Fury is cruel, and anger is
a flood,
but who can withstand
jealousy?

5 Better an open reprimand
than concealed love.

6 The wounds of a friend are
trustworthy,
but the kisses of an enemy are
excessive.

7 A person who is full tramples
on a honeycomb,
but to a hungry person, any
bitter thing is sweet.

8 A man wandering from his
home

is like a bird wandering from
its nest.

⁹ Oil and incense bring joy to the
heart,
and the sweetness of a friend is
better than self-counsel.

¹⁰ Don't abandon your friend or
your father's friend,
and don't go to your brother's
house
in your time of calamity;
better a neighbor nearby than a
brother far away.

¹¹ Be wise, my son, and bring my
heart joy,
so that I can answer anyone
who taunts me.

¹² The sensible see danger and
take cover;
the foolish keep going and are
punished.

¹³ Take his garment,
for he has put up security for
a stranger;
get collateral if it is for
foreigners.

¹⁴ If one blesses his neighbor
with a loud voice early in the
morning,
it will be counted as a curse to
him.

¹⁵ An endless dripping on a rainy
day
and a nagging wife are alike.

¹⁶ The one who controls her
controls the wind
and grasps oil with his right
hand.

¹⁷ Iron sharpens iron,
and one man sharpens
another.

¹⁸ Whoever tends a fig tree will
eat its fruit,
and whoever looks after his
master will be honored.

¹⁹ As the water reflects the face,
so the heart reflects the
person.

²⁰ Sheol and Abaddon are never
satisfied,
and people's eyes are never
satisfied.

²¹ Silver is [tested] in a crucible,
gold in a smelter,
and a man, by the praise he
receives.

²² Though you grind a fool
in a mortar with a pestle along
with grain,
you will not separate his
foolishness from him.

²³ Know well the condition of
your flock,
and pay attention to your
herds,

²⁴ for wealth is not forever;
not even a crown lasts for all
time.

25 When hay is removed and new
  growth appears
and the grain from the hills is
  gathered in,
26 lambs will provide your
  clothing,
and goats, the price of a field;
27 there will be enough goat's
  milk for your food—
food for your household
and nourishment for your
  servants.

28 The wicked flee when no one
  is pursuing [them],
but the righteous are as bold as
  a lion.

2 When a land is in rebellion, it
  has many rulers,
but with a discerning and
  knowledgeable person, it
  endures.

3 A destitute leader who
  oppresses the poor
is like a driving rain that leaves
  no food.

4 Those who reject the law praise
  the wicked,
but those who keep the law
  battle against them.

5 Evil men do not understand
  justice,
but those who seek the LORD
  understand everything.

6 Better a poor man who lives
  with integrity

than a rich man who distorts
  right and wrong.

7 A discerning son keeps the law,
but a companion of gluttons
  humiliates his father.

8 Whoever increases his wealth
  through excessive interest
collects it for one who is kind
  to the poor.

9 Anyone who turns his ear away
  from hearing the law—
even his prayer is detestable.

10 The one who leads the upright
  into an evil way
will fall into his own pit,
but the blameless will inherit
  what is good.

11 A rich man is wise in his own
  eyes,
but a poor man who has
  discernment sees through him.

12 When the righteous triumph,
  there is great rejoicing,
but when the wicked come to
  power,
people hide themselves.

13 The one who conceals his sins
  will not prosper,
but whoever confesses and
  renounces them
will find mercy.

14 Happy is the one who is always
  reverent,

but one who hardens his heart
  falls into trouble.

¹⁵ A wicked ruler over a helpless
  people
  is like a roaring lion or a
  charging bear.

¹⁶ A leader who lacks
  understanding
  is very oppressive,
  but one who hates unjust gain
  prolongs his life.

¹⁷ A man burdened by bloodguilt
  will be a fugitive until death.
  Let no one help him.

¹⁸ The one who lives with
  integrity will be helped,
  but one who distorts right and
  wrong
  will suddenly fall.

¹⁹ The one who works his land
  will have plenty of food,
  but whoever chases fantasies
  will have his fill of poverty.

²⁰ A faithful man will have many
  blessings,
  but one in a hurry to get rich
  will not go unpunished.

²¹ It is not good to show
  partiality—
  yet a man may sin for a piece
  of bread.

²² A greedy man is in a hurry
  for wealth;

he doesn't know that poverty
  will come to him.

²³ One who rebukes a person will
  later find more favor
  than one who flatters
  with his tongue.

²⁴ The one who robs his father or
  mother
  and says, "That's no sin,"
  is a companion to a man who
  destroys.

²⁵ A greedy person provokes
  conflict,
  but whoever trusts in the
  LORD will prosper.

²⁶ The one who trusts in himself
  is a fool,
  but one who walks in wisdom
  will be safe.

²⁷ The one who gives to the poor
  will not be in need,
  but one who turns his eyes away
  will receive many curses.

²⁸ When the wicked come to
  power,
  people hide,
  but when they are destroyed,
  the righteous flourish.

29

One who becomes stiff-necked,
  after many reprimands
  will be broken suddenly—
  and without a remedy.

² When the righteous flourish,

the people rejoice,
but when the wicked rule,
people groan.

3 A man who loves wisdom
brings joy to his father,
but one who consorts with
prostitutes destroys his
wealth.

4 By justice a king brings
stability to a land,
but a man [who demands]
"contributions"
demolishes it.

5 A man who flatters his
neighbor
spreads a net for his feet.

6 An evil man is caught by sin,
but the righteous one sings
and rejoices.

7 The righteous person knows
the rights of the poor,
but the wicked one does not
understand these concerns.

8 Mockers inflame a city,
but the wise turn away anger.

9 If a wise man goes to court
with a fool,
there will be ranting and
raving but no resolution.

10 Bloodthirsty men hate an
honest person,
but the upright care about him.

11 A fool gives full vent to his
anger,
but a wise man holds it in
check.

12 If a ruler listens to lies,
all his servants will be wicked.

13 The poor and the oppressor
have this in common:
the LORD gives light to the
eyes of both.

14 A king who judges the poor
with fairness—
his throne will be established
forever.

15 A rod of correction imparts
wisdom,
but a youth left to himself
is a disgrace to his mother.

16 When the wicked increase,
rebellion increases,
but the righteous will see their
downfall.

17 Discipline your son, and he
will give you comfort;
he will also give you delight.

18 Without revelation people run
wild,
but one who keeps the law will
be happy.

19 A servant cannot be
disciplined by words;
though he understands, he
doesn't respond.

²⁰ Do you see a man who speaks
  too soon?
  There is more hope for a fool
  than for him.

²¹ A slave pampered from his
  youth
  will become arrogant later on.

²² An angry man stirs up conflict,
  and a hot-tempered man
  increases rebellion.

²³ A person's pride will humble
  him,
  but a humble spirit will gain
  honor.

²⁴ To be a thief's partner is to hate
  oneself;
  he hears the curse but will not
  testify.

²⁵ The fear of man is a snare,
  but the one who trusts in the
  LORD is protected.

²⁶ Many seek a ruler's favor,
  but a man receives justice
  from the LORD.

²⁷ An unjust man is detestable to
  the righteous,
  and one whose way is upright
  is detestable to the wicked.

THE WORDS OF AGUR

30 The words of Agur son of
Jakeh. The oracle.

The man's oration to Ithiel,
  to Ithiel and Ucal:

² I am the least intelligent of
  men,
  and I lack man's ability to
  understand.

³ I have not gained wisdom,
  and I have no knowledge of the
  Holy One.

⁴ Who has gone up to heaven
  and come down?
  Who has gathered the wind in
  His hands?
  Who has bound up the waters
  in a cloak?
  Who has established all the
  ends of the earth?
  What is His name,
  and what is the name of His
  Son—
  if you know?

⁵ Every word of God is pure;
  He is a shield to those who take
  refuge in Him.

⁶ Don't add to His words,
  or He will rebuke you, and you
  will be proved a liar.

⁷ Two things I ask of You;
  don't deny them to me before
  I die:

⁸ Keep falsehood and deceitful
  words far from me.
  Give me neither poverty nor
  wealth;
  feed me with the food I need.

⁹ Otherwise, I might have too
  much
  and deny You, saying,
  "Who is the LORD?"

or I might have nothing and
steal,
   profaning the name of my God.

¹⁰ Don't slander a servant to his
master,
   or he will curse you, and you
   will become guilty.

¹¹ There is a generation that
curses its father
   and does not bless its mother.
¹² There is a generation that is
pure in its own eyes,
   yet is not washed from its filth.
¹³ There is a generation—how
haughty its eyes
   and pretentious its looks.
¹⁴ There is a generation whose
teeth are swords,
   whose fangs are knives,
   devouring the oppressed from
   the land
   and the needy from among
   mankind.

¹⁵ The leech has two daughters:
Give, Give.
   Three things are never
   satisfied;
   four never say, "Enough!":
¹⁶ Sheol; a barren womb;
   earth, which is never satisfied
   with water;
   and fire, which never says,
   "Enough!"

¹⁷ As for the eye that ridicules a
father
   and despises obedience to a
   mother,

may ravens of the valley pluck
it out
   and young vultures eat it.

¹⁸ Three things are beyond me;
   four I can't understand:
¹⁹ the way of an eagle in the sky,
   the way of a snake on a rock,
   the way of a ship at sea,
   and the way of a man with a
   young woman.

²⁰ This is the way of an adulteress:
   she eats and wipes her mouth
   and says, "I've done nothing
   wrong."

²¹ The earth trembles under three
things;
   it cannot bear up under four:
²² a servant when he becomes
king,
   a fool when he is stuffed with
   food,
²³ an unloved woman when she
marries,
   and a serving girl when she
   ousts her lady.

²⁴ Four things on earth are small,
   yet they are extremely wise:
²⁵ the ants are not a strong
people,
   yet they store up their food in
   the summer;
²⁶ hyraxes are not a mighty
people,
   yet they make their homes in
   the cliffs;
²⁷ locusts have no king,
   yet all of them march in ranks;

²⁸ a lizard can be caught in your
hands,
yet it lives in kings' palaces.

²⁹ Three things are stately in their
stride,
even four are stately in their
walk:
³⁰ a lion, which is mightiest
among beasts
and doesn't retreat before
anything,
³¹ a strutting rooster, a goat,
and a king at the head of his
army.

³² If you have been foolish by
exalting yourself,
or if you've been scheming,
put your hand over your
mouth.
³³ For the churning of milk
produces butter,
and twisting a nose draws
blood,
and stirring up anger produces
strife.

THE WORDS OF LEMUEL

31 The words of King Lemuel,
an oracle that his mother
taught him:

² What [should I say], my son?
What, son of my womb?
What, son of my vows?
³ Don't spend your energy on
women
or your efforts on those who
destroy kings.
⁴ It is not for kings, Lemuel,
it is not for kings to drink wine
or for rulers [to desire] beer.
⁵ Otherwise, they will drink,
forget what is decreed,
and pervert justice for all the
oppressed.
⁶ Give beer to one who is dying,
and wine to one whose life is
bitter.
⁷ Let him drink so that he can
forget his poverty
and remember his trouble no
more.
⁸ Speak up for those who have
no voice,
for the justice of all who are
dispossessed.
⁹ Speak up, judge righteously,
and defend the cause of the
oppressed and needy.

IN PRAISE OF A CAPABLE WIFE

¹⁰ Who can find a capable wife?
She is far more precious than
jewels.
¹¹ The heart of her husband trusts
in her,
and he will not lack anything
good.
¹² She rewards him with good,
not evil,
all the days of her life.
¹³ She selects wool and flax
and works with willing hands.
¹⁴ She is like the merchant ships,
bringing her food from far
away.
¹⁵ She rises while it is still night
and provides food for her
household
and portions for her servants.

16 She evaluates a field and buys it;
   she plants a vineyard with her earnings.
17 She draws on her strength
   and reveals that her arms are strong.
18 She sees that her profits are good,
   and her lamp never goes out at night.
19 She extends her hands to the spinning staff,
   and her hands hold the spindle.
20 Her hands reach out to the poor,
   and she extends her hands to the needy.
21 She is not afraid for her household when it snows,
   for all in her household are doubly clothed.
22 She makes her own bed coverings;
   her clothing is fine linen and purple.
23 Her husband is known at the city gates,
   where he sits among the elders of the land.
24 She makes and sells linen garments;
   she delivers belts to the merchants.
25 Strength and honor are her clothing,
   and she can laugh at the time to come.
26 She opens her mouth with wisdom,
   and loving instruction is on her tongue.
27 She watches over the activities of her household
   and is never idle.
28 Her sons rise up and call her blessed.
   Her husband also praises her:
29 "Many women are capable,
   but you surpass them all!"
30 Charm is deceptive and beauty is fleeting,
   but a woman who fears the LORD will be praised.
31 Give her the reward of her labor,
   and let her works praise her at the city gates.

National Distributors

UK: (and countries not listed below)
CWR, Waverley Abbey House, Waverley Lane, Farnham, Surrey GU9 8EP.
Tel: (01252) 784700 Outside UK (44) 1252 784700 Email: mail@cwr.org.uk

AUSTRALIA: KI Entertainment, Unit 21 317-321 Woodpark Road, Smithfield, New South Wales 2164.
Tel: 1 800 850 777 Fax: 02 9604 3699 Email: sales@kientertainment.com.au

CANADA: David C Cook Distribution Canada, PO Box 98, 55 Woodslee Avenue, Paris, Ontario N3L 3E5.
Tel: 1800 263 2664 Email: swansons@cook.ca

GHANA: Challenge Enterprises of Ghana, PO Box 5723, Accra. Tel: (021) 222437/223249
Fax: (021) 226227 Email: ceg@africaonline.com.gh

HONG KONG: Cross Communications Ltd, 1/F, 562A Nathan Road, Kowloon.
Tel: 2780 1188 Fax: 2770 6229 Email: cross@crosshk.com

INDIA: Crystal Communications, 10-3-18/4/1, East Marredpalli, Secunderabad – 500026,
Andhra Pradesh. Tel/Fax: (040) 27737145 Email: crystal_edwj@rediffmail.com

KENYA: Keswick Books and Gifts Ltd, PO Box 10242-00400, Nairobi. Tel: (254) 20 312639/3870125
Email: keswick@swiftkenya.com

MALAYSIA: Salvation Book Centre (M) Sdn Bhd, 23 Jalan SS 2/64, 47300 Petaling Jaya, Selangor.
Tel: (03) 78766411/78766797 Fax: (03) 78757066/78756360 Email: info@salvationbookcentre.com
Canaanland, No. 25 Jalan PJU 1A/41B, NZX Commercial Centre, Ara Jaya, 47301 Petaling Jaya, Selangor.
Tel: (03) 7885 0540/1/2 Fax: (03) 7885 0545 Email: info@canaanland.com.my

NEW ZEALAND: KI Entertainment, Unit 21 317-321 Woodpark Road, Smithfield, New South Wales
2164, Australia. Tel: 0 800 850 777 Fax: +612 9604 3699 Email: sales@kientertainment.com.au

NIGERIA: FBFM, Helen Baugh House, 96 St Finbarr's College Road, Akoka, Lagos.
Tel: (01) 7747429/4700218/825775/827264 Email: fbfm@hyperia.com

PHILIPPINES: OMF Literature Inc, 776 Boni Avenue, Mandaluyong City.
Tel: (02) 531 2183 Fax: (02) 531 1960 Email: gloadlaon@omflit.com

SINGAPORE: Alby Commercial Enterprises Pte Ltd, 95 Kallang Avenue #04-00, AIS Industrial Building,
339420. Tel: (65) 629 27238 Fax: (65) 629 27235 Email: marketing@alby.com.sg

SOUTH AFRICA: Struik Christian Books, 80 MacKenzie Street, PO Box 1144, Cape Town 8000.
Tel: (021) 462 4360 Fax: (021) 461 3612 Email: info@struikchristianmedia.co.za

SRI LANKA: Christombu Publications (Pvt) Ltd, Bartleet House, 65 Braybrooke Place, Colombo 2.
Tel: (9411) 2421073/2447665 Email: dhanad@bartleet.com

USA: David C Cook Distribution Canada, PO Box 98, 55 Woodslee Avenue, Paris, Ontario N3L 3E5,
Canada. Tel: 1800 263 2664 Email: swansons@cook.ca

Day and Residential Courses
Counselling Training
Leadership Development
Biblical Study Courses
Regional Seminars
Ministry to Women
Daily Devotionals
Books and DVDs
Conference Centre

Trusted all Over the World

CWR HAS GAINED A WORLDWIDE
reputation as a centre of excellence for
Bible-based training and resources. From
our headquarters at Waverley Abbey House,
Farnham, England, we have been serving
God's people for over 40 years with a vision
to help apply God's Word to everyday life and
relationships. The daily devotional *Every Day
with Jesus* is read by nearly a million readers
an issue in more than 150 countries, and our
unique courses in biblical studies and pastoral
care are respected all over the world. Waverley
Abbey House provides a conference centre in a
tranquil setting.

For free brochures on our seminars and
courses, conference facilities, or a catalogue
of CWR resources, please contact us at the
following address.
CWR, Waverley Abbey House, Waverley Lane,
Farnham, Surrey GU9 8EP, UK

Telephone: **+44 (0)1252 784700**
Email: **mail@cwr.org.uk**
Website: **www.cwr.org.uk**

CWR Applying God's Word
to everyday life and relationships

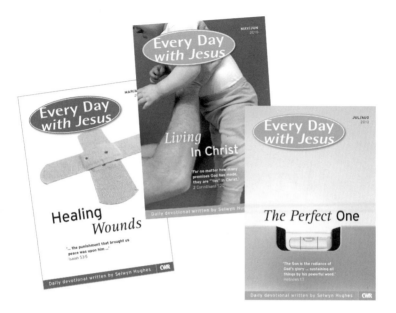

Meet with Jesus through His Word each day

Drawing on fifty years of pastoral and counselling experience, Selwyn Hughes has authored one of the most popular daily Bible study tools in the world, with around one million readers.

- Get practical help with life's challenges
- Gain insight into the deeper truths of Scripture
- Be challenged, comforted and encouraged
- Study six topics in depth each year.

170x120mm booklet
ISSN: 0967-1889
£2.49 per issue
£13.80 six issues per year, published bimonthly

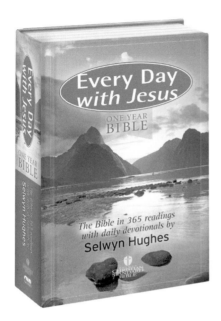

Variety in a one-year Bible-reading programme

With 365 daily readings from both Testaments, plus excerpts from the Psalms and
Proverbs, our *Every Day with Jesus One Year Bible* provides a deeply enriching
way to read through the Bible in a year.

Each day's Scripture passage is made more relevant to you by devotional
comments from Selwyn Hughes, a brief prayer and probing questions.

Why not get your church to read the Bible together in a year? Bulk discounts are
available for churches!

1,632-page, hardback with ribbon marker
ISBN: 978-1-85345-342-7
£14.99

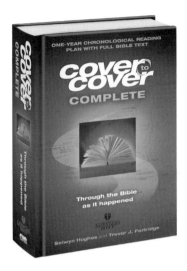

Read the whole Bible in a year, chronologically

The Bible is an epic story with numerous twists, turns and sub-plots, but its length and complexity mean many Christians struggle to read it in its entirety.

Cover to Cover Complete makes Bible reading easy by breaking down the entire Bible into 366 fifteen-minute daily readings, arranged in chronological order. Beautiful charts, maps, illustrations and diagrams make the biblical background vivid, timelines enable you to track your progress, and daily commentary helps you apply what you read to your life.

Why not get your church to read the Bible together in a year? Bulk discounts are available for churches!

Selwyn Hughes and Trevor J. Partridge
1,600-page hardback
ISBN: 978-1-85345-433-2
£19.99